Exercises to Lesson One

Exercise 1-A: Copy the words below, using the space provided at the right of each:

1. κατα	____________	10. πασα	____________
2. συν	____________	11. παντοτε	____________
3. ποθεν	____________	12. κωλυω	____________
4. θελω	____________	13. δουλευω	____________
5. γραμμα	____________	14. μορφη	____________
6. χαρις	____________	15. σοφος	____________
7. λαθρα	____________	16. δογμα	____________
8. βαπτιζω	____________	17. καλυφω	____________
9. ψυχη	____________	18. ζωη	____________

Exercise 1-B: Transliterate the following into Roman (English) letters, using the space provided at the right of each:

1. θεος	____________	6. παθος	____________
2. στιγμα	____________	7. χαρακτηρ	____________
3. λαρυγξ	____________	8. βαπτιζω	____________
4. ζωνη	____________	9. νεος	____________
5. φαρμακον	____________	10. τεχνη	____________

Exercise 1-C: Transliterate the following pairs of words into Greek letters:

1. ton	______	5. nēthō	______
tou	______	nēphō	______
2. ton	______	6. kopos	______
tōn	______	koros	______
3. zōē	______	7. dexomai	______
zōn	______	dechomai	______
4. grapsō	______	8. krazō	______
graphō	______	kraxō	______

Exercise 1-D: Transliterate the following words into Greek capital letters:

1. KAINĒ	______	9. TAPHEI	______
2. DIATHĒKĒ	______	10. MATHEIN	______
3. KOINON	______	11. MOICHEIA	______
4. BEBAION	______	12. MARTYRIA	______
5. KATOIKIZEIN	______	13. TAXIN	______
6. GALILAIA	______	14. KYRIOS	______
7. PSEUDOS	______	15. CHRISTOS	______
8. BAPTIZONTA	______	16. IĒSOUS	______

Exercises to Lesson Two

Exercise 2-A: Write the following "minimal pairs" (i.e., pairs of words which contrast in only one particular). This is a dictation exercise, and should be done in class. The instructor should vary the order of the words in the pairs, and should repeat any that are difficult for the student. (One "run" of the exercise may be made with this sheet, if desired, with the student covering the Greek column and writing in the spaces provided.)

1.	κόσμον	__________	8.	ἔξω	__________
	κόσμων	__________		ἕξω	__________
2.	νῦν	__________	9.	ἔθους	__________
	νοῦν	__________		ἤθους	__________
3.	αὐτό	__________	10.	ἀρχῶν	__________
	αὐτά	__________		ἀρκῶν	__________
4.	σωτῆρος	__________	11.	λῖτρα	__________
	σωτῆρας	__________		λύτρα	__________
5.	ἄρσεν	__________	12.	ἄρκων	__________
	ἄρσην	__________		ἄρχων	__________
6.	ἑστός	__________	13.	χαλῶν	__________
	ἑστώς	__________		καλῶν	__________
7.	ἀληθής	__________	14.	δέ	__________
	ἀληθές	__________		δή	__________

ω = ōmega
o = ŏmicron

Exercise 2-B: Dictation exercise. In view of the lack of contrast, the instructor may divide the words in this exercise into two groups, the first of which does not contain η, and the second of which does not contain ει. (Neither contains an iota subscript.)

(a)
1. θεός ____________
2. κύριος ____________
3. πνεῦμα ____________
4. ἀδελφός ____________
5. σάρξ ____________
6. βασιλεία ____________
7. ἄγγελος ____________
8. ἄγκυρα ____________
9. σπλάγχνα ____________
10. λάρυγξ ____________

(b)
1. καινή ____________
2. διαθήκη ____________
3. προφήτης ____________
4. χάρις ____________
5. ἅγιος ____________
6. δόξα ____________
7. βαπτίζω ____________
8. ὕψιστος ____________
9. σῶμα ____________
10. εὕρηκα ____________

Exercise 2-C: Groups (a) and (b) are again divided as above.

(a)
1. βδέλυγμα ____________
2. σβεννύειν ____________
3. θλῖψις ____________
4. πτύειν ____________
5. κτίσις ____________
6. μνεία ____________
7. σθενοῦν ____________
8. φθόγγος ____________

(b)
1. γνώμη ____________
2. πτωχός ____________
3. ζωή ____________
4. θνητός ____________
5. σφόδρα ____________
6. σχῆμα ____________
7. φθάνω ____________
8. ψυχή ____________

9. Χριστός	________	9. χλαμύς	________
10. ψεῦδος	________	10. μνημονεύω	________

Exercise 2-D: Transliterate into English letters:

1. εὐαγγέλιον	________	6. σάλπιγξ	________
2. ἑρμηνευτής	________	7. οἰκονομία	________
3. παραλυτικός	________	8. ὑγίεια	________
4. ἱερόν	________	9. ἀνάθεμα	________
5. ἑπτά	________	10. ἀποστασία	________

Exercise 2-E: Transliterate into Greek letters:

1. enkaínia	________	6. élenchos	________
2. exḗgēsis	________	7. oikouménē	________
3. paráklētos	________	8. Hērṓidēs	________
4. rhḗtōr	________	9. hýdōr	________
5. hēgemonía	________	10. eucharistía	________

Exercise 2-F: Copy and memorize:

Πάτερ ἡμῶν ὁ ἐν τοῖς οὐρανοῖς·
Ἁγιασθήτω τὸ ὄνομά σου·
ἐλθάτω ἡ βασιλεία σου·
γενηθήτω τὸ θέλημά σου,
ὡς ἐν οὐρανῷ καὶ ἐπὶ γῆς·
Τὸν ἄρτον ἡμῶν τὸν ἐπιούσιον δὸς ἡμῖν σήμερον·
καὶ ἄφες ἡμῖν τὰ ὀφειλήματα ἡμῶν,
ὡς καὶ ἡμεῖς ἀφήκαμεν τοῖς ὀφειλέταις ἡμῶν·
καὶ μὴ εἰσενέγκῃς ἡμᾶς εἰς πειρασμόν,
ἀλλὰ ῥῦσαι ἡμᾶς ἀπὸ τοῦ πονηροῦ. Ἀμήν.

W 6

Exercises to Lesson Three

Exercise 3-A: In the following pairs of sentences one or more letters of a word have been underlined. Indicate, by striking out the inappropriate words at the right, (a) whether these words represent the same or different sounds, and (b) whether they represent the same or different morphemes. (The procedure to be followed is illustrated first.)

0. Thrifty housewives can tomatoes.	same ~~different~~ sound
Thrifty housewives can save money.	~~same~~ different morpheme
1. The boys ran quickly.	same different sound
The boy's hat blew off.	same different morpheme
2. She wished to come soon.	same different sound
She wanted to come soon.	same different morpheme
3. She loves him.	same different sound
She hates him.	same different morpheme
4. She charms everyone.	same different sound
Her charms are fading.	same different morpheme
5. He flembers the boxes.	same different sound
Our flembers are absent.	same different morpheme

Exercise 3-B: Underline the words in the list below in which -er does not represent a morpheme:

1. writer
2. cover

3. lover

4. under

5. thunder

6. squander

7. commander

8. salamander

9. ladder

10. sadder

Exercise 3-C: If the underlined portions of the words at the left are forms of the same morpheme, put an X in the first ( ) at the right; if they are not forms of the same morpheme, put an X in the second ( ):

			Same Morpheme	Not same Morpheme
1.	kinder	grinder	( )	( )
2.	greater	grater	( )	( )
3.	sixth	seventh	( )	( )
4.	third	thirteen	( )	( )
5.	friendship	steamship	( )	( )
6.	countess	princess	( )	( )
7.	knife	knives	( )	( )
8.	childish	dish	( )	( )
9.	reaped	wept	( )	( )
10.	antidote	antedate	( )	( )

Exercise 3-D: Describe briefly the meaning associated with the underlined morphemes (the same morpheme is underlined in each word or phrase in a group, although it may have variant forms):

1. hats, gloves, oxen ______________________________

2. he comes, she goes, it hurts ______________________________

____

3. I wanted, you slept, they raised

4. greater, kinder, taller

5. speaker, builder, writer

6. brutalize, civilize, humanize

7. defrost, decompose, desegregate

8. kindness, awkwardness, politeness

9. sixteen, seventeen, eighteen

10. unwelcome, undo, unfaithful

Exercise 3-E: Study the following Greek verb-forms with their English equivalents:

γράφομεν	we write	ἀκούω	I hear
ἐγράφομεν	we were writing	ἀκούσω	I shall hear
κρίνετε	you (plural) judge	λύω	I loose
κρίνεις	you (singular) judge	λύσω	I shall loose
ἐκρίνατε	you (pl.) judged	λύσετε	you (pl.) will loose
ἔκρινας	you (sg.) judged	ἔλυες	you (sg.) were loosing

The following meanings are expressed by morphemes in the Greek forms:

(a) I as "doer of the action"
(b) you (sg.) as "doer of the action"
(c) you (pl.) as "doer of the action"
(d) we as "doer of the action"
(e) past time
(f) future time

Fill in the blanks at the right below with the letters indicating the meanings just listed:

1. The suffix μεν is associated with meaning _____
2. The suffix τε " " " " _____
3. The suffix ω " " " " _____
4. The suffix ς " " " " _____
5. The infix σ " " " " _____
6. The prefix ἐ " " " " _____

(Note: Prefixes, infixes, and suffixes are morphemes occurring at the beginning, middle, and end of words.)

Exercises to Lesson Four

Exercise 4-A: What grammatical devices are misused in the following sentences (i.e., from the standpoint of "standard" English)?

1. I don't like those kind of apples.

____

2. Between you and I, I think he's crazy.

____

3. Whom do you think you are?

____

4. Me wants a new toy!

____

5. A list of rules are posted on the bulletin board.

____

Exercise 4-B: What grammatical devices are used in English to indicate questions? Illustrate your answer by referring to the following sentences:

1. (a) She is here.
   (b) She is here?
   (c) Is she here?
2. (a) She has arrived.
   (b) Has she arrived?
3. (a) He has the money.
   (b) Has he the money?
   (c) Does he have the money?
4. (a) She pays rent.
   (b) Does she pay rent?
5. (a) They can swim.
   (b) Can they swim?
6. (a) She paid too much.
   (b) Did she pay too much?
7. (a) What did you see?
   (b) Who came?
   (c) When are you going?

Do any of these devices occur only with certain verbs, or only with certain kinds of verbs? Explain your answer below:

____

____

____

____

____

____

____

____

____

____

____

____

____

____

____

____

____

____

____

____

____

____

____

____

Exercise 4-C: Any of the Greek sentences at the left below may be translated by either of the English sentences at the right. What devices does English use to express the structural meaning "indirect object"? (The "indirect object" indicates the "person to or for which something is done".) What device does Greek use, so far as you can judge from this exercise?

Vocabulary:	ἔδωκε	he gave
	δοῦλος	a slave
	νόμος	a law

ἔδωκε δούλῳ νόμον
ἔδωκε νόμον δούλῳ
δούλῳ ἔδωκε νόμον
δούλῳ νόμον ἔδωκε
νόμον δούλῳ ἔδωκε
νόμον ἔδωκε δούλῳ

= He gave a slave a law.
He gave a law to a slave.

Answer in this space:

____

____

____

____

____

____

____

____

<u>Exercise 4-D</u>: The Greek function words ὑπό, σύν, and πρός correspond (fairly closely) in meaning to English <u>by</u>, <u>with</u>, and <u>to</u>. From the phrases given below, how would you say the Greek function words differ from the English ones?

by God = ὑπὸ θεοῦ

with God = σὺν θεῷ

to God = πρὸς θεόν

Answer in this space: ______________________________

Exercises to Lesson Five

Exercise 5-A: Using either the inflectional or distributional method of classification (described in Pars. 33(1),(2)), assign the underlined nonsense words to parts of speech:

1. The flembers are good. Part of speech ____________
   Dictionary form ____________
2. She is flember than he is. Part of speech ____________
   Dictionary form ____________
3. He flembered it rather badly. Part of speech ____________
   Dictionary form ____________
4. 'Twas brillig, and the slithy toves
   Did gyre and gimble in the wabe;
   All mimsy were the borogoves,
   And the mome raths outgrabe.

(In answering this question proceed as follows: "Brillig here occupies a position which might be occupied by early or late; early and late are adjectives, since we can say The early bird was early and The late train was late. Therefore, brillig is an adjective." More than one classification may be possible for some forms.)

Part of speech:

brillig = ____________

slithy = ____________

toves = ____________

gyre = ____________

gimble = ____________

wabe = ____________

mimsy = ____________

borogoves = ____________

mome = ____________

raths = ____________

outgrabe = ____________

<u>Exercise 5-B</u>: On the basis of the model paradigms in Par. 34, give the <u>dictionary form</u> of each of the following nouns. If more than one dictionary form is possible, give all of them. Then look up the words in a dictionary, underline the correct dictionary form (if you have found more than one to be theoretically possible), and give the meaning of the word (the first meaning listed will be sufficient here).

		Meaning
1. ἄγγελον	____________	________
2. μαθητήν	____________	________
3. ἀδελφοί	____________	________
4. ἀνθρώπους	____________	________
5. ἁμαρτίαν	____________	________
6. εἰρήνην	____________	________
7. θάνατον	____________	________
8. διδαχαί	____________	________

<u>Exercise 5-C</u>: Write the accusative singular, nominative plural, and accusative plural of each of the following words in the spaces provided:

Nominative Singular	Accusative Singular	Nominative Plural	Accusative Plural
1. βασιλεία	________	________	________
2. τόπος	________	________	________
3. προφήτης	________	________	________
4. φωνή	________	________	________
5, δόξα	________	________	________

Exercises to Lesson Six

Exercise 6-A: The Vocabulary below may be used in this exercise (the meanings, however, are not really needed):

ὁ θεός	God	ἡ ψυχή	the soul
ὁ δοῦλος	the slave	ἡ χήρα	the widow
ὁ μαθητής	the disciple	ἡ ἄμπελος	the vine
		τὸ τέκνον	the child

Supply the form of the article which is grammatically appropriate in the blank space in each sentence below:

1. ἀγαπᾷ ὁ θεὸς _____ χήραν.
2. ἀγαπᾷ ὁ θεὸς _____ δούλους.
3. ἀγαπᾷ ὁ θεὸς _____ τέκνον.
4. ἀγαπᾷ ὁ θεὸς _του_ μαθητήν.
5. ἀγαπᾷ ὁ θεὸς _____ ἄμπελον.
6. ἀγαπᾷ ὁ θεὸς _____ μαθητάς.
7. ἀγαπᾷ ὁ θεὸς _____ ψυχήν.
8. ἀγαπᾷ ὁ θεὸς _____ τέκνα.
9. ἀγαπᾷ ὁ θεὸς _____ δοῦλον.
10. ἀγαπᾷ ὁ θεὸς _____ χήρας.
11. ἀγαπᾷ τὸ τέκνον _____ θεός.
12. ἀγαπᾷ τὸ τέκνον _____ θεόν.
13. ἀγαπᾷ τὸ τέκνον _____ ἀμπέλους.
14. ἀγαπᾷ τὸ τέκνον _____ μαθητής.
15. ἀγαπῶσιν τὰ τέκνα _____ μαθηταί.
16. ἀγαπῶσιν τὰ τέκνα _____ δοῦλοι.
17. ἀγαπῶσιν τὰ τέκνα _____ δοῦλον.
18. ἀγαπῶσιν τὰ τέκνα _____ χήρας.
19. ἀγαπῶσιν τὰ τέκνα _____ χῆραι.
20. ἀγαπῶσιν τὰ τέκνα _____ χήραν.

Exercise 6-B: Put an X in the ( ) before the word at the right which can fill the blank in the sentence:

1. τὸν ________ ἀγαπᾷ ὁ θεὸς.

( ) τέκνον

( ) δοῦλον

( ) ἄμπελον

( ) χήραν

2. τοὺς ________ ἀγαπᾷ ὁ θεὸς.

( ) ψυχάς

( ) τέκνα

( ) ἀμπέλους

( ) μαθητάς

3. τὰ ________ ἀγαπᾷ ὁ θεὸς.

( ) τέκνα

( ) χήρα

( ) ἄμπελον

( ) ψυχή

4. τὴν ________ ἀγαπᾷ ὁ θεὸς.

( ) μαθητήν

( ) δοῦλον

( ) τέκνα

( ) ἄμπελον

<u>Exercise 6-C</u>: Below is a list of Greek nouns of the first and second declensions in various cases and numbers (other than the nominative singular). By inspection, determine the dictionary form and look it up in a dictionary. (Give the proper form of the article with the dictionary form.)

	Dictionary form	Meaning
1. τοὺς ἀποστόλους	____________	____________
2. τὰς ἐντολάς	____________	____________
3. τὴν ἐξουσίαν	____________	____________
4. τὴν ζωήν	____________	____________
5. τὴν θάλασσαν	____________	____________
6. τὸν καιρόν	____________	____________
7. τὰ πρόβατα	____________	____________
8. αἱ φωναί	____________	____________
9. οἱ ἐργάται	____________	____________
10. αἱ ἔρημοι	____________	____________

Exercises to Lesson Seven

Exercise 7-A: Underline the subjects and doubly underline the direct objects in the sentences below. To what extent is your ability to recognize the subjects and objects dependent on the meanings of the words?

1. My alembic needs a new cucurbit.
2. Deep machicolations separated the corbels of the parapet.
3. The porbeagle devoured the poor beagle.
4. Her battledore struck the shuttlecock.
5. The hawker hooded his lanneret.

Exercise 7-B: Underline the subjects and doubly underline the direct objects in the sentences below:

1. τὸν νόμον ἱστάνει ὁ ἀπόστολος.
2. τὴν ἀλήθειαν ἐρεῖ ὁ μαθητής.
3. σοφίαν οἱ ἀπόστολοι λαλοῦσι.
4. ἠγάπησεν ὁ θεὸς τὸν κόσμον.
5. ἡ ἀγάπη ἐκβάλλει τὸν φόβον.
6. τὰς ἐντολὰς οἱ πιστοὶ τηροῦσι.
7. ἐξουσίαν ἔχει ὁ υἱός.
8. ἡ γῆ ἐβλάστησεν τὸν καρπόν.
9. ὁ κύριος ἦρεν τοὺς ὀφθαλμούς.
10. πρόσωπον ὁ θεὸς οὐ λαμβάνει.

<u>Exercise 7-C</u>: Study the sentences in Par. 50; then, without referring to a dictionary, give the dictionary form (in Greek, with the article) for each of the following:

1. the earth	____________	5. the fruit	____________
2. the tree	____________	6. the world	____________
3. the bridegroom	____________	7. (the) God	____________
4. the son	____________	8. the steward	____________

(The dictionary forms of the other nouns in the sentences in Par. 50, with their articles, are given below:)

the power	ἡ ἐξουσία
the vine	ἡ ἄμπελος
the man	ὁ ἄνθρωπος

<u>Exercise 7-D</u>: Referring to the previous exercise, give the Greek <u>nominative plural</u> forms corresponding to the English nouns below:

1. the trees	____________	5. the sons	____________
2. the bridegrooms	____________	6. the gods	____________
3. the fruits	____________	7. the powers	____________
4. the vines	____________	8. the men	____________

(The proper form of the <u>article</u> should be given with each of the above.)

Exercise 7-E: Referring to the sentences in Par. 50 and the two exercises on page W 22, translate the following into Greek:

1. The man has sons. ______________________________

2. God calls the steward.

____

3. The bridegroom planted a tree.

____

Exercise 7-F: Fill in the blank in each Greek sentence (with Greek words in the appropriate case) so that it will be a translation of the English sentence which precedes it:

1. The earth brought forth the trees.
ἡ γῆ ἐβλάστησεν ______________________________

2. The earth brought forth vines.
ἀμπέλους ἐβλάστησεν ______________________________

3. The vine brought forth the fruit.
τὸν καρπὸν ἐβλάστησεν ______________________________

4. A man planted the tree.
ἐφύτευσεν ἄνθρωπος ______________________________

5. God loved the earth.
ἠγάπησεν ὁ θεὸς ______________________________

6. The man has power.
ὁ ἄνθρωπος ἔχει ______________________________

7. The world has power.
ἐξουσίαν ἔχει ______________________________

8. God has a son.

υἱὸν ὁ θεὸς ____________

9. The bridegroom calls the men.

φωνεῖ ὁ νυμφίος ____________________

10. The man loved God.

ἠγάπησεν ὁ ἄνθρωπος ________________

Exercises to Lesson Eight

Exercise 8-A: Underline the subjects and doubly underline the predicate nominatives in the sentences below. (English translations are given at the right.)

1. οἱ θερισταὶ ἄγγελοί εἰσιν. (Cf. Mt 13:39) — The reapers are angels.
2. θεὸς ἦν ὁ λόγος. (Cf. Jn 1:1) — The Word was God.
3. ἡ σοφία μωρία ἐστίν. (Cf. 1 Cor 3:19) — The wisdom is foolishness.
4. Ἰάκωβος καὶ Ἰωάννης ἦσαν κοινωνοί. (Cf. Lk 5:10) — James and John were partners.
5. αἱ λυχνίαι ἐκκλησίαι εἰσίν. (Cf. Rev 1:20) — The lampstands are churches.
6. οἱ ἄνθρωποι δοῦλοί εἰσιν. (Cf. Acts 16:17) — The men are slaves.

Exercise 8-B: Study the sentences in the exercise above, and give the dictionary form (in Greek, with the article) for the following: (Use a dictionary if you wish.)

1. the reaper ______________
2. the word ______________
3. the foolishness ______________
4. the church ______________
5. the angel ______________
6. the wisdom ______________
7. the lampstand ______________
8. the slave ______________
9. the partner ______________

<u>Exercise 8-C</u>: From the sentences in Exercise 8-A, determine the Greek equivalents for the following English verb-forms:

(Note: The Greek forms are for the third person only, as indicated by the pronouns in parentheses.)

1. (he, she, it) is ________ 3. (he, she, it) was ________
2. (they) are ________ 4. (they) were ________

<u>Exercise 8-D</u>: Refer to the Exercises to Lesson Seven and to the preceding exercises in the present lesson, and fill in the blank in each Greek sentence below so that it will be a translation for the English sentence which precedes it:

1. The angels are reapers. οἱ ἄγγελοι ______________ εἰσιν.
2. The angel is a reaper. ὁ ἄγγελος ______________ ἐστιν.
3. The man was a slave. ὁ ἄνθρωπος ______________ ἦν.
4. The man has a slave. ὁ ἄνθρωπος ______________ ἔχει.
5. The church is a lampstand. ______________ λυχνία ἐστίν.
6. The church has a lampstand. ______________ λυχνίαν ἔχει.
7. The men were partners. ______________ κοινωνοὶ ἦσαν.
8. The man has a partner. ______________ κοινωνὸν ἔχει.
9. The words are foolishness. ______________ εἰσὶν οἱ λόγοι.
10. The world loved foolishness. ______________ ἠγάπησεν ὁ κόσμος.

Exercises to Lesson Nine

Exercise 9-A: (Class Question.) Why need not the ending of an adjective be the same as the ending of the noun it modifies? (See Par. 68, and explain the examples there.)

The following Vocabulary may be used in connection with Exercise 9-B:

Adjectives		Nouns	
ἀγαθός, ή, όν,	good	ὁ ἄνθρωπος,	man
δίκαιος, α, ον,	righteous, just	ὁ κύριος,	lord
πονηρός, ά, όν,	evil, wicked	ἡ ἡμέρα,	day
αἰώνιος, ον,	eternal	ἡ ἀγάπη,	love
ἀγαπητός, ή, όν,	beloved	τὸ ἔργον,	work
ἅγιος, α, ον,	holy	ὁ μαθητής,	disciple
καινός, ή, όν.	new	ὁ ἄγγελος,	angel
νεκρός, ά, όν,	dead	ἡ ὁδός,	way
πιστός, ή, όν,	faithful	ὁ ἀδελφός,	brother

Exercise 9-B: Put an X in the ( ) before the Greek expressions at the right below which correctly render the English expressions to the left of them:

1. The good man.
   ( ) καλὸς ὁ ἄνθρωπος
   ( ) ὁ ἄνθρωπος καλός
   ( ) ὁ καλὸς ἄνθρωπος

2. The righteous lord.
   ( ) ὁ κύριος ὁ δίκαιος
   ( ) ὁ κύριος δίκαιος
   ( ) δίκαιος ὁ κύριος

3. The days are evil.

( ) αἱ πονηραὶ ἡμέραι
( ) αἱ ἡμέραι πόνηραί
( ) αἱ ἡμέραι αἱ πονηραί

4. The eternal love.

( ) αἰώνιος ἡ ἀγάπη
( ) ἡ αἰωνία ἀγάπη
( ) ἡ ἀγάπη ἡ αἰώνιος

5. The work is holy.

( ) ἅγιον τὸ ἔργον
( ) τὸ ἅγιον ἔργον
( ) τὸ ἔργον τὸ ἅγιον

6. The beloved disciple.

( ) ὁ μαθητὴς ὁ ἀγαπητής
( ) ὁ μαθητὴς ὁ ἀγαπητός
( ) ὁ μαθητὴς ἡ ἀγαπητός

7. The angels are holy.

( ) ἅγιοι οἱ ἄγγελοι
( ) οἱ ἅγιοι ἄγγελοι
( ) οἱ ἄγγελοι οἱ ἅγιοι

8. The new way.

( ) ἡ ὁδὸς ἡ καινός
( ) ἡ ὁδὸς ὁ καινή
( ) ἡ ὁδὸς ἡ καινή

9. The brothers are dead.

( ) οἱ ἀδελφοὶ νεκροί
( ) οἱ νεκροὶ ἀδελφοί
( ) οἱ ἀδελφοὶ οἱ νεκροί

10. The disciples are faithful.

( ) οἱ μαθηταὶ πισταί
( ) οἱ μαθηταὶ πιστοί
( ) οἱ μαθηταὶ οἱ πισταί

11. The works are evil.

( ) τὰ πονηρὰ ἔργα
( ) πονηρὰ τὰ ἔργα
( ) τὰ ἔργα τὰ πονηρά

12. The dead are beloved.

( ) οἱ νεκροὶ ἀγαπητοί
( ) νεκροὶ οἱ ἀγαπητοί
( ) οἱ ἀγαπητοὶ νεκροί

13. The lord is righteous.

( ) δίκαιος ὁ κύριος
( ) κύριος ὁ δίκαιος
( ) ὁ κύριος ὁ δίκαιος

14. The righteous are faithful.

( ) πιστοὶ οἱ δίκαιοι
( ) δίκαιοι οἱ πιστοὶ
( ) οἱ πιστοὶ δίκαιοι

15. The eternal lord.

( ) ὁ αἰώνιον κύριος
( ) ὁ κύριος αἰώνιος
( ) ὁ αἰώνιος κύριος

Exercise 9-C: So that the Greek sentences below will correctly translate the accompanying English sentences, fill in the blank spaces with (a) the proper forms of καλός, ή, όν, good, and (b), if necessary, also the proper forms of the article (that is, some blanks require only a form of καλός, while others require a form of the article and a form of καλός):

1. The good earth brought forth the fruit.
   ἡ ____________ γῆ ἐβλάστησεν τὸν καρπόν.

2. The good earth brought forth the fruit.
   ἡ γῆ _________________ ἐβλάστησεν τὸν καρπόν.

3. The earth is good.
   ἡ γῆ ________________

4. The earth brought forth the good fruit.
   ἡ γῆ ἐβλάστησεν τὸν καρπὸν ____________________

5. The lord calls the good slaves.
   φωνεῖ τοὺς ________________ δούλους ὁ κύριος.

6. The slaves are good.
   ________________ οἱ δοῦλοι.

7. A man planted the good tree.
   τὸ __________________ δένδρον ἄνθρωπος ἐφύτευσεν.

8. The trees are good.
   τὰ δένδρα _________________

Exercises to Lesson Ten

Exercise 10-A: Fill in the forms of the genitive (G) and accusative (A) singular and of the nominative, genitive, and accusative plural in the paradigms below, supplying the proper form of the article in each case:

First Declension

Feminine

Sg.N. ἡ διαθήκη

G. ________________

A. ________________

Pl.N. ________________

G. ________________

A. ________________

Feminine

Sg.N. ἡ δόξα

G. ________________

A. ________________

Pl.N. ________________

G. ________________

A. ________________

Feminine

Sg.N. ἡ ἐκκλησία

G. ________________

A. ________________

Pl.N. ________________

G. ________________

A. ________________

Masculine

Sg.N. ὁ μαθητής

G. ________________

A. ________________

Pl.N. ________________

G. ________________

A. ________________

First Declension Nouns with Adjectives of the First and Second Declensions

Sg.N. ὁ καλὸς προφήτης

G. ______________________________

A. ______________________________

Pl.N. ______________________________

G. ______________________________

A. ______________________________

Sg.N. ἡ δικαία χήρα

G. ______________________________

A. ______________________________

Pl.N. ______________________________

G. ______________________________

A. ______________________________

Second Declension

Masculine

Sg.N. ὁ δοῦλος

G. ____________________

A. ____________________

Pl.N. ____________________

G. ____________________

A. ____________________

Feminine

Sg.N. ἡ ὁδός

G. ____________________

A. ____________________

Pl.N. ____________________

G. ____________________

A. ____________________

Neuter

Sg.N. τὸ τέκνον

G. ____________________

A. ____________________

Pl.N. ____________________

G. ____________________

A. ____________________

Exercise 10-B: (In this exercise, "nouns" means "nouns of the first and second declensions", unless further restricted.) Basing your answers on the illustrative expressions in Par. 73, indicate whether the following statements are true or false by placing T or F in the parentheses at the right of each:

1. The genitive singular of all first declension nouns ends in -ης. ( )
2. The genitive plural of all nouns ends in -ων. ( )
3. The genitive singular of all second declension nouns ends in -ου. ( )
4. The genitive singular of all first declension feminine nouns ends in -ης. ( )
5. The genitive singular of all masculine nouns ends in -ου. ( )
6. If a noun has the ending -ου, it is in the genitive. ( )
7. If a noun has the ending -ης, it is in the genitive. ( )
8. Some feminine nouns have the ending -ου in the genitive. ( )
9. Some masculine nouns have the ending -ης in the genitive. ( )
10. If the nominative singular of a first declension noun ends in -α its genitive singular ends in -ας. ( )
11. The genitive plural of all first declension nouns ends in -ῶν (with the circumflex accent). ( )
12. When an adjective modifies a noun, it always has the same ending as the noun has. ( )

Exercise 10-C: In each of the three statements below, strike out the words which do not apply:

1. τῆς is the genitive singular plural
masculine feminine or neuter form of the article.

2. τοῦ is the genitive singular plural
masculine or feminine or neuter form of the article.

3. τῶν is the genitive singular plural
masculine or feminine or neuter form of the article.

Exercise 10-D: Supply the endings as indicated by the model provided:

	Singular			Plural		
	N	G	A	N	G	A
1.	ὁ κύριος	ου	ον	οι	ων	ους
2.	ἡ ἡμέρα					
3.	ἡ ἁμαρτία					
4.	ἡ φωνή					
5.	τὸ δένδρον					
6.	ὁ προφήτης					
7.	ἡ θάλασσα					
8.	ἡ ἄμπελος					

<u>Exercise 10-E</u>: Refer to the Vocabulary in Par. 73 and translate the following into English:

1. ὁ τῆς ἐκκλησίας μαθητής.

____

2. ἡ τοῦ μαθητοῦ ἐκκλησία.

____

3. τὸ τέκνον τὸ τοῦ δούλου.

____

4. ἡ δόξα ἡ τῆς διαθήκης.

____

5. ἡ τῆς δόξης διαθήκη.

____

6. ἡ ἐκκλησία ἡ τῶν μαθητῶν.

____

7. ἡ ὁδὸς τῆς δόξης.

____

8. ἡ τῆς ὁδοῦ δόξα.

____

9. τὰ τῶν δούλων τέκνα.

____

10. αἱ τῶν διαθηκῶν ὁδοί.

____

Exercise 10-F: Refer to the two model sentences which are given below with their English translations, and then translate the remaining Greek sentences into English:

(A) ὁ τοῦ μαθητοῦ ἀδελφὸς βλέπει τὸν δοῦλον τὸν τῆς χήρας.

The disciple's brother sees the widow's slave.

(B) τὸν τῆς χήρας δοῦλον οἱ ἀδελφοὶ τοῦ μαθητοῦ βλέπουσιν.

The disciple's brothers see the widow's slave.

1. βλέπει τὸν τοῦ δούλου μαθητὴν ἡ χήρα ἡ τοῦ ἀδελφοῦ.

____

2. τοὺς ἀδελφοὺς τοὺς τῶν δούλων βλέπουσιν αἱ τῶν μαθητῶν χῆραι.

____

3. ὁ τοῦ μαθητοῦ δοῦλος βλέπει τὴν χήραν τοῦ ἀδελφοῦ.

____

4. ὁ μαθητὴς ὁ τοῦ ἀδελφοῦ τοὺς τῶν χηρῶν δούλους βλέπει.

____

5. τὸν τῆς χήρας δοῦλον ὁ ἀδελφὸς ὁ τοῦ μαθητοῦ βλέπει.

____

Exercises to Lesson Eleven

Exercise 11-A: Fill in the forms of the genitive (G), dative (D), and accusative (A) singular, and of the nominative, genitive, dative and accusative plural in the paradigms below, supplying the proper form of the article in each case:

First Declension

Feminine		Feminine	
Sg.N.	ἡ ἀδελφή	Sg.N.	ἡ βασίλισσα
G.	________	G.	________
D.	________	D.	________
A.	________	A.	________
Pl.N.	________	Pl.N.	________
G.	________	G.	________
D.	________	D.	________
A.	________	A.	________

Feminine		Masculine	
Sg.N.	ἡ χήρα	Sg.N.	ὁ προφήτης
G.	________	G.	________
D.	________	D.	________
A.	________	A.	________
Pl.N.	________	Pl.N.	________
G.	________	G.	________
D.	________	D.	________
A.	________	A.	________

Second Declension

Masculine

Sg.N. ὁ δοῦλος

G. ____________

D. ____________

A. ____________

Pl.N. ____________

G. ____________

D. ____________

A. ____________

Feminine

Sg.N. ἡ τροφός

G. ____________

D. ____________

A. ____________

Pl.N. ____________

G. ____________

D. ____________

A. ____________

Neuter

Sg.N. τὸ τέκνον

G. ____________

D. ____________

A. ____________

Pl.N. ____________

G. ____________

D. ____________

A. ____________

First and Second Declension Nouns with Adjectives of the First and Second Declensions

Sg.N. ὁ δίκαιος προφήτης
G. ______
D. ______
A. ______

Pl.N. ______
G. ______
D. ______
A. ______

Sg.N. ὁ κακὸς δοῦλος
G. ______
D. ______
A. ______

Pl.N. ______
G. ______
D. ______
A. ______

Sg.N. ἡ πονηρὰ τροφός
G. ______
D. ______
A. ______

Pl.N. ______
G. ______
D. ______
A. ______

Sg.N. τὸ καλὸν τέκνον
G. ______
D. ______
A. ______

Pl.N. ______
G. ______
D. ______
A. ______

<u>Exercise 11-B</u>: (In this exercise, "nouns" means "nouns of the first and second declensions", unless further restricted.) Basing your answers on the illustrative sentences in Par. 81, indicate whether the following statements are true or false by placing T or F in the parentheses at the right of each:

1. The dative singular of all nouns has iota subscript. ( )
2. The dative singular of all first declension nouns ends in -ῃ or -ᾳ. ( )
3. The dat. sg. of all masculine nouns ends in -ῳ. ( )
4. The dat. sg. of all second declension nouns ends in -ῳ. ( )
5. The dat. sg. of all feminine nouns ends in -ῃ or -ᾳ. ( )
6. The dat. pl. of all masculine nouns ends in -οις. ( )
7. The dat. pl. of all feminine nouns ends in -αις. ( )
8. The dat. pl. of all first declension nouns ends in -αις. ( )
9. The dat. pl. of all second declension nouns ends in -οις. ( )
10. A noun in the dat. case may come anywhere in the sentence. ( )

Exercise 11-C: In each of the statements below, strike out the words which do not apply:

1. τῷ is the dative singular plural
masculine or feminine or neuter form of the article.

2. τῇ is the dative singular plural
masculine or feminine or neuter form of the article.

3. τοῖς is the dative singular plural
masculine or feminine or neuter form of the article.

4. ταῖς is the dative singular plural
masculine or feminine or neuter form of the article.

Exercise 11-D: Give the correct endings, imitating the Model given:

	Singular				Plural			
	N	G	D	A	N	G	D	A
Model:	ὁ κόσμ-ος	ου	ῳ	ον	οι	ων	οις	ους
1.	ἡ ψυχ-ή							
2.	τὸ ἱμάτι-ον							
3.	ἡ γλῶσσ-α							
4.	ὁ λόγ-ος							
5.	ἡ θυσί-α							
6.	ἡ κιβωτ-ός							
7.	ἡ στο-ά							
8.	ὁ δεσπότ-ης							

Exercise 11-E: Supply the proper form of the proper word in the blank spaces in the Greek sentences which follow, so that each will be a translation of the English sentence which precedes it. A short Vocabulary is provided:

ἀδελφός, οῦ, ὁ,	brother
βασιλεία, ας, ἡ,	kingdom
γῆ, ῆς, ἡ,	land
ἐντολή, ῆς, ἡ,	commandment
Ἰησοῦς, οῦ, ὁ,	Jesus (see Par. 82)
Ἰούδας, α, ὁ,	Judas (see Par. 82)
κύριος, ου, ὁ,	lord, Lord, master
ὁδός, οῦ, ἡ,	way
τέκνον, οῦ, τό,	child

(Note: The proper form of the article should be supplied with each noun, including the proper names.)

1. Jesus gave the prophet joy.

   χαρὰν τῷ προφήτῃ ἔδωκεν ______________________

2. The prophet saw Jesus.

   εἶδεν ὁ προφήτης ______________________

3. Jesus gave the sop to Judas.

   ἔδωκεν τὸ ψωμίον ὁ Ἰησοῦς ______________________

4. The disciple of the Lord came.

   ἦλθεν ὁ μαθητὴς ______________________

5. The brothers are faithful.

   πιστοὶ ______________________

6. The man saw the brothers.

   εἶδεν ὁ ἄνθρωπος ______________________

7. The disciple is faithful to the way of the Lord.

ὁ μαθητὴς πιστὸς ______________ τοῦ κυρίου.

8. The ways of the Lord are holy.

ἅγιαι ______________ τοῦ κυρίου.

9. The disciple knew the ways of the Lord.

ἔγνωκεν ὁ μαθητὴς ______________ τοῦ κυρίου.

10. The child has a sister.

ἀδελφὴν ἔχει ______________

11. The sister has children.

ἔχει ἡ ἀδελφὴ ______________

12. The man gave the children the loaves.

ὁ ἄνθρωπος τοὺς ἄρτους ἔδωκεν ______________

13. The earth is good.

καλὴ ______________

14. The Lord gave the commandment to men.

ἀνθρώποις ἔδωκεν ὁ κύριος ______________

15. The disciples are faithful to the commandments.

οἱ μαθηταὶ πιστοὶ ______________

16. The kingdom of God is good.

καλὴ ______________ τοῦ θεοῦ.

17. The disciple saw the kingdom of Jesus.

εἶδεν ὁ μαθητὴς τὴν βασιλείαν ______________

18. The disciple gave Jesus glory.

ἔδωκεν ὁ μαθητὴς δόξαν ______________

19. Judas gave the disciples sorrow.

ἔδωκεν λύπην τοῖς μαθηταῖς ______________

20. Jesus knew the sin of Judas.

ἔγνωκεν ὁ Ἰησοῦς τὴν ἁμαρτίαν ____________________

21. God gave laws for the kingdoms.

νόμους ἔδωκεν ὁ θεὸς ________________________

22. The law of the commandments is just.

δίκαιος ὁ νόμος _____________________________

23. The Lord of the earth is good.

καλὸς ὁ κύριος _____________

24. The sister gave the child the fruit.

ἔδωκεν ἡ ἀδελφὴ τὸν καρπὸν __________________

25. The sister of the child is faithful.

πιστὴ ἡ ἀδελφὴ ____________________

Exercises to Lesson Twelve

Exercise 12-A: (a) Write out the full paradigm for the verb λύω in the present indicative active (the numbers indicate first, second, and third persons):

Singular	Plural
1. ________	1. ________
2. ________	2. ________
3. ________	3. ________

(b) Write out the full paradigm for the verb γράφω in the present indicative active:

Singular	Plural
1. ________	1. ________
2. ________	2. ________
3. ________	3. ________

Exercise 12-B: (a) Write out the full paradigm for the verb λύω in the future indicative active:

Singular	Plural
1. ________	1. ________
2. ________	2. ________
3. ________	3. ________

(b) Write out the full paradigm for the verb γράφω in the future indicative active:

Singular	Plural
1. ________	1. ________
2. ________	2. ________
3. ________	3. ________

Exercise 12-C: Change each of the following forms to the corresponding form of the future tense (i.e., retain the same person and number):

1. θεραπεύω	________	6. καθίζεις	________
2. γνωρίζει	________	7. στρέφομεν	________
3. κρύπτετε	________	8. πράσσω	________
4. διώκουσιν	________	9. λούει	________
5. κτίζομεν	________	10. ἥκετε	________

Exercise 12-D: Using the vocabulary given, translate the English into Greek:

Vocabulary

λύω,	I loose	διώκω,	I pursue, I persecute
ἀκούω,	I hear	πέμπω,	I send
γράφω,	I write	ἄγω,	I lead
βαπτίζω,	I baptize	πείθω,	I persuade

1. You (sg.) are loosing ____________
2. He hears ____________
3. We are sending ____________
4. You (pl.) will be writing ____________
5. He will persuade ____________
6. You (pl.) will persecute ____________
7. You (sg.) will baptize ____________
8. They will send ____________
9. We shall lead ____________
10. They are writing ____________

<u>Exercise 12-E</u>: Put an X in the ( ) before the verb-form which will be grammatically appropriate in the blank space in the sentence to the left of it:

1. τοὺς δούλους ὁ προφήτης __________ ( ) λύετε
( ) λύουσιν
( ) λύσει
( ) λύσουσιν

2. οἱ δοῦλοι τὴν βασίλισσαν __________ ( ) λύουσιν
( ) λύεις
( ) λύσει
( ) λύει

3. τὰς ἁμαρτίας τοῦ λαοῦ ὁ θεὸς ____________ ( ) καλύπτουσιν
( ) καλύψετε
( ) καλύψει
( ) καλύπτεις

4. τοὺς τυφλοὺς ______________ ὁ Ιησοῦς. ( ) θεραπεύουσιν
( ) θεραπεύσει
( ) θεραπεύσουσιν
( ) θεραπεύετε

5. ____________ τὸν ἀπόστολον αἱ ἐκκλησίαι· ( ) πέμπεις
( ) πέμπει
( ) πέμψει
( ) πέμψουσιν

6. ________________ τὰ τέκνα τὸν κύριον. ( ) δοξάζομεν
( ) δοξάζετε
( ) δοξάζει
( ) δοξάζεις

Exercises to Lesson Thirteen

Exercise 13-A: Fill in the table below, imitating the model given; retain the person and number of the given form, but change the tense as indicated (all the forms of this exercise are to be obtained by the rules given in Lessons 12-13; all of the aorists required are first aorists):

Present	Imperfect	Future	Aorist
λύω	ἔλυον	λύσω	ἔλυσα
1. δοξάζει			
2. λάμπομεν			
3. ἀλείφεις			
4. φυλάσσετε			
5. παύουσιν			
6. ὁδεύω			

Exercise 13-B: Fill in the table below; all of the aorist forms required in this exercise are second aorists.

Present	Imperfect	Future	Aorist
1. λείπει			
2. ἄγουσιν			
3. εὑρίσκεις			
4. ἔχει [1]			
5. ἁμαρτάνετε			

[1] See Par. 95(4),(7) for the imperfect, future, and aorist of this verb.

Exercise 13-C: Put an X in each of the appropriate spaces in the table below, imitating the model given. (The only second aorist forms in this table are those of verbs which appear in Par. 95(7)).

	Person			Number		Tense			
	1	2	3	Sg.	Pl.	Pres.	Impf.	Fut.	Aor.
Model: κηρύσσεις		X		X		X			
1. ἠκούσαμεν									
2. ἡτοίμαζεν									
3. ἐκήρυσσεν									
4. ἀγοράζομεν									
5. ἐκηρύξαμεν									
6. ἄξετε									
7. διώξετε									
8. ἔχομεν									
9. ἡτοίμασαν									
10. ἠγοράσατε									
11. ἔσχετε									
12. διώκουσιν									
13. ἀγοράσει									
14. ἀκούσουσιν									
15. εἴχετε									
16. δοξάσει									
17. βαπτίζει									
18. ἐδίωκες									
19. ἤκουεν									
20. ἐλίπομεν									
21. ἤγαγεν									
22. γράφει									
23. ἐπέμψαμεν									
24. εὗρες									
25. ἔγραψα									
26. ἐπέμπομεν									
27. γράψει									
28. πιστεύετε									
29. βαπτίσεις									
30. ἐλείπομεν									

Exercise 13-D: Supply the proper verb-forms in the blank spaces in the Greek sentences below so that each will be a translation of the English sentence which precedes it. (Imitate the model provided before each group of sentences.)

Model: The apostle is preaching the gospel.
ὁ ἀπόστολος τὸ εὐαγγέλιον κηρύσσει.

1. The apostle will preach the gospel.
ὁ ἀπόστολος τὸ εὐαγγέλιον ________________

2. The apostles were preaching the gospel.
οἱ ἀπόστολοι τὸ εὐαγγέλιον ________________

3. You (pl.) have preached the gospel.
τὸ εὐαγγέλιον ____________________

4. They used to preach the gospel.
τὸ εὐαγγέλιον ____________________

5. We shall preach the gospel.
τὸ εὐαγγέλιον ___________________

Model: The disciple is preparing the way.
ὁ μαθητὴς τὴν ὁδὸν ἑτοιμάζει.

6. The disciple was preparing the way.
ὁ μαθητὴς τὴν ὁδὸν ________________

7. We have prepared the way.
τὴν ὁδὸν _____________

8. The disciples will prepare the way.
οἱ μαθηταὶ τὴν ὁδὸν ______________

9. You (sg.) are preparing the way.
τὴν ὁδὸν ____________________

10. The disciples are preparing the way.
    οἱ μαθηταὶ τὴν ὁδὸν ________________

Model: The church is sending a disciple.
    ἡ ἐκκλησία μαθητὴν πέμπει.

11. The church has sent a disciple.
    ἡ ἐκκλησία μαθητὴν ________________

12. The church will send disciples.
    ἡ ἐκκλησία μαθητὰς ________________

13. They used to send disciples.
    μαθητὰς ________________

14. I was sending disciples.
    μαθητὰς ________________

15. We shall be sending disciples.
    μαθητὰς ________________

Model: The prophet is writing a law.
    ὁ προφήτης νόμον γράφει.

16. The prophets were writing a law.
    οἱ προφῆται νόμον ________________

17. The prophet used to write laws.
    ὁ προφήτης νόμους ________________

18. The prophet has written a law.
    ὁ προφήτης νόμον ________________

19. We shall write laws.
    νόμους ________________

20. You (sg.) have written a law.
    νόμον ________________

Model: The child has the bread.

τὸ τέκνον τὸν ἄρτον ἔχει.

21. The child has had the bread.

τὸ τέκνον τὸν ἄρτον ______________

22. The children shall have the bread.

τὰ τέκνα τὸν ἄρτον ________________

23. The children used to have the bread.

τὰ τέκνα τὸν ἄρτον ________________

24. We have the bread.

τὸν ἄρτον ________________

25. You (pl.) have had the bread.

τὸν ἄρτον ________________

Model: The Lord is leading the disciples.

ὁ κύριος τοὺς μαθητὰς ἄγει.

26. The Lord will lead the disciples.

ὁ κύριος τοὺς μαθητὰς _________

27. They were leading the disciples.

τοὺς μαθητὰς ______________

28. You (pl.) were leading the disciples.

τοὺς μαθητὰς ______________

29. You (pl.) are leading the disciples.

τοὺς μαθητὰς ______________

30. You (pl.) have led the disciples.

τοὺς μαθητὰς ______________

<u>Model</u>: The apostle is baptizing the slaves.
ὁ ἀπόστολος τοὺς δούλους βαπτίζει.

31. The apostle has baptized the slaves.
ὁ ἀπόστολος τοὺς δούλους ____________________

32. The apostles were baptizing the slaves.
οἱ ἀπόστολοι τοὺς δούλους ____________________

33. We shall baptize the slaves.
τοὺς δούλους ______________

34. They will baptize the slaves.
τοὺς δούλους _______________

35. You (sg.) are baptizing the slaves.
τοὺς δούλους ______________

<u>Model</u>: The soldier is pursuing a widow.
ὁ στρατιώτης χήραν διώκει.

36. The soldier was pursuing a widow.
ὁ στρατιώτης χήραν _____________

37. The soldier will pursue the slave.
ὁ στρατιώτης τὸν δοῦλον __________

38. The soldiers have pursued the slaves.
οἱ στρατιῶται τοὺς δούλους ___________________

39. They will pursue the soldier.
τὸν στρατιώτην _______________

40. We are pursuing the soldiers.
τοὺς στρατιώτας ______________

Exercises to Lesson Fourteen

Exercise 14-A: Indicate whether the following statements are true or false, by placing T or F in the ( ) at the right of each:

1. In the paradigms of (a) οὗτος and (b) the definite article, the rough breathing occurs on corresponding forms. ( )
2. In the paradigm of οὗτος the diphtong αυ occurs in the first syllable of all feminine forms. ( )
3. In the paradigm of οὗτος the diphtong αυ occurs in some masculine forms. ( )
4. In the paradigm of οὗτος the diphtong αυ occurs in some neuter forms. ( )
5. In the paradigm of οὗτος the diphtong αυ occurs in the first syllable only in forms whose endings contains α or η. ( )
6. The endings of οὗτος are the same as those of the article. ( )
7. The endings of οὗτος are the same as those of αὐτός. ( )
8. The endings of οὗτος are the same as those of ἐκεῖνος. ( )
9. Οὗτος sometimes occurs in first attributive position. ( )
10. Αὐτός sometimes occurs in first attributive position. ( )

<u>Exercise 14-B</u>: Place an X in the ( ) <u>before</u> the expression which correctly completes the statement:

1. In the construction οὗτος ὁ κύριος, οὗτος is in ( ) the first attributive position ( ) the second attributive position ( ) the first predicate position ( ) the second predicate position ( ) none of the positions just named.
2. In the construction το τέκνον αὐτό, αὐτό is in ( ) the first attributive position ( ) the second attributive position ( ) the first predicate position ( ) none of the positions just named.
3. In the construction τοῦτο ποτήριόν ἐστιν, τοῦτο is in ( ) the first attributive position ( ) the second attributive position ( ) the first predicate position ( ) the second predicate position ( ) none of the positions just named.
4. In the construction ὁ αὐτὸς μαθητής, αὐτός is in ( ) the first attributive position ( ) the second attributive position ( ) the first predicate position ( ) the second predicate position ( ) none of the positions just named.
5. In the construction ὁ μαθητὴς τοῦ κυρίου, τοῦ κυρίου is in ( ) the first attributive position ( ) the second attributive position ( ) the first predicate position ( ) the second predicate position ( ) none of the positions just named.

Exercise 14-C: In the blank spaces in the Greek sentences below, insert (a) the correct form of οὗτος, αὐτός or ἐκεῖνος, and (b) if necessary, the correct form of the article so that the Greek will correctly render the English which precedes it. Imitate the models provided:

Model (i): This disciple sent the child.
ἔπεμψεν τὸ τέκνον οὗτος ὁ μαθητής (οὗτος ὁ supplied)

Model (ii): This disciple sent the child.
ἔπεμψεν τὸ τέκνον ὁ μαθητὴς οὗτος. (οὗτος supplied)

1. The disciple sent this child.
ἔπεμψεν ὁ μαθητὴς ________________ τέκνον.

2. The disciple sent this child.
ἔπεμψεν ὁ μαθητὴς τὸ τέκνον ______________

3. The disciple sent the child to this widow.
ἔπεμψεν ὁ μαθητὴς τὸ τέκνον τῇ χήρᾳ _____________

4. These disciples sent the child.
ἔπεμψαν τὸ τέκνον οἱ μαθηταὶ _____________

5. The same disciple sent the child.
ἔπεμψεν τὸ τέκνον ________________ μαθητής.

6. That disciple sent the child.
ἔπεμψεν τὸ τέκνον ὁ μαθητὴς ______________

7. The widow of this disciple sent the child.
ἔπεμψεν τὸ τέκνον ἡ χήρα ________________ μαθητοῦ.

8. The widow herself sent the child.
ἔπεμψεν τὸ τέκνον ______________ χήρα.

9. The child of that widow sent the disciple.
   ἔπεμψεν τὸν μαθητὴν τὸ τέκνον ________________ χήρας.

10. These children sent the disciple.
    ἔπεμψαν τὸν μαθητὴν τὰ τέκνα ________________

11. Those children sent the disciple.
    ἔπεμψαν τὸν μαθητὴν ____________________ τέκνα.

12. The same children sent the disciple.
    ἔπεμψαν τὸν μαθητὴν ____________________ τέκνα.

13. The children themselves sent the disciple.
    ἔπεμψαν τὸν μαθητὴν ____________________ τέκνα.

14. The child of that good widow sent the disciple.
    ἔπεμψεν τὸν μαθητὴν τὸ τέκνον τῆς καλῆς χήρας _____________

15. The disciple sent the child to the same widow.
    ἔπεμψεν τὸ τέκνον ὁ μαθητὴς ________________ χήρᾳ.

16. The disciple sent the child of the same widow.
    ἔπεμψεν ὁ μαθητὴς τὸ τέκνον ______________ χήρας.

17. The disciples themselves sent the children.
    ἔπεμψαν τὰ τέκνα οἱ μαθηταὶ ________________

18. The disciples sent the children of those widows.
    ἔπεμψαν οἱ μαθηταὶ τὰ τέκνα τῶν χηρῶν _____________

19. That child sent the disciple.
    ἔπεμψεν τὸν μαθητὴν ____________________ τέκνον.

20. The widow sent the child to that disciple.
    ἔπεμψεν ἡ χήρα τὸ τέκνον τῷ μαθητῇ ________________

Exercises to Lesson Fifteen

Exercise 15-A: Fill in the blank spaces with the proper form of αὐτός so that the Greek sentences will correctly render the English ones which precede them.

Note: A pronoun in the exercises should have the gender of the corresponding noun in the preceding model. (All subject pronouns are to be expressed.)

Model A: The apostle told the disciple the parable.
ὁ ἀπόστολος ἐλάλησεν τῷ μαθητῇ τὴν παραβολήν.

1. He told the disciple the parable.
_____________ ἐλάλησεν τὴν παραβολήν τῷ μαθητῇ.

2. The apostle told him the parable.
ὁ ἀπόστολος ἐλάλησεν _______________ τὴν παραβολήν.

3. The apostle told it to the disciple.
ὁ ἀπόστολος ἐλάλησεν _______________ τῷ μαθητῇ.

4. The apostle told the parable to him.
ὁ ἀπόστολος _______________ ἐλάλησεν τὴν παραβολήν.

Model B: The sister knows the child.
ἡ ἀδελφὴ τὸ τέκνον γινώσκει.

5. She knows the child.
_________ τὸ τέκνον γινώσκει.

6. The sister knows him.
__________ ἡ ἀδελφὴ γινώσκει.

Model C: The disciples sent the children to the apostles.
οἱ μαθηταὶ ἔπεμψαν τὰ τέκνα τοῖς ἀποστόλοις.

7. They sent the children to the apostles.
__________ τὰ τέκνα τοῖς ἀποστόλοις ἔπεμψαν.

8. The disciples sent them the children.
______________ ἔπεμψαν οἱ μαθηταὶ τὰ τέκνα.

9. The disciples sent them to the apostles.
____________ ἔπεμψαν οἱ μαθηταὶ τοῖς ἀποστόλοις.

Model D: The slaves of the widow are the disciples of the Lord.
οἱ δοῦλοι τῆς χήρας εἰσὶν οἱ μαθηταὶ τοῦ κυρίου.

10. Her slaves are the Lord's disciples.
οἱ δοῦλοι _____________ εἰσὶν οἱ μαθηταὶ τοῦ κυρίου.

11. Her slaves are his disciples.
οἱ ___________ δοῦλοί εἰσιν _____________ οἱ μαθηταὶ.

12. They are his disciples.
____________ εἰσιν οἱ μαθηταὶ ___________

Model E: The Lord of the disciples is the foundation of the church.
ὁ κύριος τῶν μαθητῶν ἐστιν ὁ θεμέλιος τῆς ἐκκλησίας.

13. Their Lord is the foundation of the church.
ὁ κύριος _______________ ἐστιν ὁ θεμέλιος τῆς ἐκκλησίας.

14. The disciples' Lord is its foundation.
ὁ τῶν μαθητῶν κύριος ἐστιν ὁ θεμέλιος ______________

15. Their Lord is its foundation.
__________ ὁ κύριος ἐστιν ___________ ὁ θεμέλιος.

Exercise 15-B: Place an X in the ( ) before the English word at the right which correctly renders the underlined Greek word in the sentence or expression at the left:

1. αὐτὸς ὁ θεὸς ἔπεμψεν τὸν υἱόν.
( ) his
( ) him
( ) himself
( ) same

2. ὁ θεὸς ἔπεμψεν τὸν <u>αὐτοῦ</u> υἱόν.

( ) same
( ) his
( ) him
( ) himself

3. οὗτός ἐστιν ὁ μαθητὴς τοῦ υἱοῦ τοῦ <u>αὐτοῦ</u>.

( ) his
( ) himself
( ) same
( ) him

4. ὁ θεὸς ἔπεμψεν <u>αὐτῷ</u> τὸν υἱόν.

( ) him
( ) his
( ) same
( ) himself

5. ὁ θεὸς ἔπεμψεν τὸν υἱὸν <u>αὐτόν</u>.

( ) him
( ) he
( ) same
( ) himself

6. <u>αὐτὸς</u> τὸν υἱὸν ἔπεμψεν.

( ) he
( ) him
( ) his
( ) same

7. <u>αὐτοῦ</u> τὸν υἱὸν ἔπεμψεν ὁ θεός.

( ) same
( ) himself
( ) his
( ) him

8. <u>οὗτος</u> ὁ θεὸς ἔπεμψεν τὸν υἱόν.

( ) same
( ) himself
( ) this
( ) his

9. ὁ θεὸς <u>αὐτοῦ</u> ἔπεμψεν τὸν υἱόν.

( ) his
( ) himself
( ) same
( ) this

10. ὁ θεὸς ἔπεμψεν τὸν <u>αὐτὸν</u> υἱόν.

( ) same
( ) his
( ) himself
( ) this

Exercise 15-C: Supply, in the space provided, the correct subject pronouns for the verb-forms below:

1. πέμπεις	__________	11. λείπομεν	__________
2. τρίψεις	__________	12. ἄξεις	__________
3. ἐγράψαμεν	__________	13. ἕξετε	__________
4. καλύπτετε	__________	14. ἥμαρτες	__________
5. διώξομεν	__________	15. ἔσχομεν	__________
6. ἤνοιξα	__________	16. εὗρες	__________
7. ἤλεγξες	__________	17. ἠγάγετε	__________
8. κηρύσσεις	__________	18. ἔπεισα	__________
9. ἤλεγχες	__________	19. ἐβαπτίσαμεν	__________
10. κηρύξομεν	__________	20. ἐσπεύσατε	__________

<u>Exercise 15-D</u>: Fill in the blank spaces with the appropriate pronouns, so that the Greek sentences will correctly render the English ones. Use the <u>unaccented</u> forms, where these exist. A model is provided to illustrate the syntax.

<u>Model</u>: The apostle sent the disciples a slave.
ὁ ἀπόστολος ἔπεμψεν δοῦλον τῷ μαθητῇ.

1. The apostle sent me to the disciple.
   ὁ ἀπόστολος τῷ μαθητῇ ἔπεμψεν ________

2. The apostle sent you (sg.) to the disciple.
   ὁ ἀπόστολος τῷ μαθητῇ ἔπεμψεν ________

3. The apostle sent us to the disciple.
   ὁ ἀπόστολος τῷ μαθητῇ ἔπεμψεν ________

4. The apostle sent you (pl.) to the disciple.
   ὁ ἀπόστολος τῷ μαθητῇ ἔπεμψεν ________

5. The apostle sent me a slave.
   ὁ ἀπόστολος δοῦλον ἔπεμψεν ________

6. The apostle sent you (sg.) a slave.
   ὁ ἀπόστολος δοῦλον ἔπεμψεν ________

7. The apostle sent us a slave.
   ὁ ἀπόστολος δοῦλον ἔπεμψεν ________

8. The apostle sent you (pl.) a slave.
   ὁ ἀπόστολος δοῦλον ἔπεμψεν ________

9. The apostle sent the disciple to us.
   ὁ ἀπόστολος τὸν μαθητὴν ἔπεμψεν ________

10. The apostle sent them to you (pl.).
    ὁ ἀπόστολος ἔπεμψεν αὐτοὺς ________

Exercise 15-E: Same instructions as for 15-D.

Model: The Lord's brothers are baptizing the prophets' disciples.
οἱ ἀδελφοὶ τοῦ κυρίου βαπτίζουσιν τοὺς μαθητὰς τῶν προφητῶν.

1. My brothers are baptizing the prophets' disciples.
τοὺς μαθητὰς τῶν προφητῶν βαπτίζουσιν οἱ ἀδελφοί ___________

2. The Lord's brothers are baptizing your (sg.) disciples.
οἱ ἀδελφοὶ τοῦ κυρίου βαπτίζουσιν τοὺς μαθητάς ___________

3. Your (pl.) brothers are baptizing the prophets' disciples.
τοὺς μαθητὰς τῶν προφητῶν βαπτίζουσιν οἱ ἀδελφοὶ ___________

4. Our brothers are baptizing the prophets' disciples.
τοὺς μαθητὰς τῶν προφητῶν βαπτίζουσιν οἱ ἀδελφοὶ ___________

5. The Lord's brothers are baptizing my disciples.
οἱ ἀδελφοὶ τοῦ κυρίου βαπτίζουσιν τοὺς μαθητάς ___________

6. Your (sg.) brothers are baptizing the prophet's disciples.
τοὺς μαθητὰς τοῦ προφήτου βαπτίζουσιν οἱ ἀδελφοί ___________

7. The Lord's brothers are baptizing our disciples.
οἱ ἀδελφοὶ τοῦ κυρίου βαπτίζουσιν τοὺς μαθητὰς ___________

8. The Lord's brothers are baptizing your (pl.) disciples.
οἱ ἀδελφοὶ τοῦ κυρίου βαπτίζουσιν τοὺς μαθητὰς ___________

9. The Lord's brothers are baptizing disciples of ours.
οἱ ἀδελφοὶ τοῦ κυρίου βαπτίζουσιν μαθητὰς ___________

10. The Lord's brothers are baptizing disciples of mine.
οἱ ἀδελφοὶ τοῦ κυρίου βαπτίζουσιν μαθητάς ___________

Exercise 15-F: Same instructions as for 15-D, but use the accented forms. (Same model as for 15-D.)

1. The apostle sent me a slave.
   __________ δοῦλον ἔπεμψεν ὁ ἀπόστολος.

2. The apostle sent you (sg.) a slave.
   __________ δοῦλον ἔπεμψεν ὁ ἀπόστολος.

3. The apostle sent a slave to me.
   __________ δοῦλον ἔπεμψεν ὁ ἀπόστολος.

4. The apostle sent me to a slave.
   __________ δούλῳ ἔπεμψεν ὁ ἀπόστολος.

5. The apostle sent you (sg.) to a slave.
   __________ δούλῳ ἔπεμψεν ὁ ἀπόστολος.

Exercise 15-G: In each of the sentences below, change the genitive of the personal pronoun to a possessive adjective in the first attributive position so that the meaning of the sentence is unchanged (copy the rest of the sentence):

1. διδάσκει τοὺς δούλους μου.

   ____

2. οἱ μαθηταί σου οὐ νηστεύουσιν.

   ____

3. ὁ καιρός μου οὔπω πεπλήρωται.

   ____

4. εἰς τὴν διδασκαλίαν ἡμῶν ἐγράφη.

   ____

5. κατὰ τὸν νόμον ἡμῶν ἠθελήσαμεν κρίνειν αὐτόν.

____

6. ἐν τῷ νόμῳ ὑμῶν γέγραπται.

____

<u>Exercise 15-H</u>: Same as Exercise 15-G, but put the possessive adjective in the <u>second</u> attributive position:

1. ἡ κρίσις μου δικαία ἐστίν.

____

2. αὗταί εἰσιν αἱ ἐντολαί μου.

____

3. ὁ λόγος σου ἀλήθειά ἐστιν.

____

4. τὸ ἔθνος σου καὶ οἱ ἀρχιερεῖς παρέδωκάν σε ἐμοί.

____

5. προσευξόμεθα ὑπὲρ τῶν ἀδελφῶν ἡμῶν.

____

6. εὐχαριστοῦμεν διὰ τὴν πίστιν ὑμῶν.

____

Exercises to Lesson Sixteen

Exercise 16-A: Examine the sentences in Par. 119, an then write out in full the paradigms of the verb λύω in the present and imperfect indicative, active and passive.

Active		Passive	
Present			
Sg.1.	________	Sg.1.	________
2.	________	2.	________
3.	________	3.	________
Pl.1.	________	Pl.1.	________
2.	________	2.	________
3.	________	3.	________
Imperfect			
Sg.1.	________	Sg.1.	________
2.	________	2.	________
3.	________	3.	________
Pl.1.	________	Pl.1.	________
2.	________	2.	________
3.	________	3.	________

Exercise 16-B: What endings must be added to the present base (here λυ-) to form the present indicative passive?

Sg.1.	________	Pl.1.	________
2.	________	2.	________
3.	________	3.	________

Exercise 16-C: What endings must be added to the augmented present base (here ἐλυ-) to form the imperfect indicative passive?

Sg.1.	______	Pl.1.	______
2.	______	2.	______
3.	______	3.	______

Exercise 16-D: Fill in the blank spaces in the table below with the missing forms, retaining the person and number of the given form. (Refer to Lessons 12 and 13, if necessary.)

	Active		Passive	
	Present	Imperfect	Present	Imperfect
1.	δοξάζεις			
2.		ἐλάμπετε		
3.			ἀλείφονται	
4.				ἐφυλάσσετο
5.	παύομεν			
6.		ἔλειπεν		
7.			ἄγομαι	
8.	ἀκούουσιν			
9.		ἐδιώκετε		
10.			ἑτοιμάζεται	
11.				ἐβαπτίζου
12.	πέμπω			
13.		ἔγραφεν		
14.			κηρύσσῃ	
15.				ἐπιστευόμην

<u>Exercise 16-E</u>: Transform the sentences with active verbs into sentences of equivalent meaning with passive verbs. Retain the tense of the verb in the given sentence, but adjust the person and number if necessary. The procedure is indicated by the model.

<u>Model</u>: ὁ προφήτης βαπτίζει τοὺς μαθητάς.

<u>Answer</u>: οἱ μαθηταὶ βαπτίζονται ὑπὸ τοῦ προφήτου.

1. ὁ ἀπόστολος ἔπεμπεν τὸν δοῦλον.

___

2. οἱ στρατιῶται τὴν χήραν διώκουσιν.

___

3. σὺ ἑτοιμάζεις τὴν ὁδόν.

___

4. ἐγὼ ἐκήρυσσον τὸ εὐαγγέλιον.

___

5. νόμους γράφομεν ἡμεῖς.

___

6. ἄγετε ὑμεῖς τοὺς μαθητάς.

___

7. αὐτὸς ἐβάπτιζεν τὸν ἄνθρωπον.

___

8. αὐτοὶ δοξάζουσιν τὸν θεόν.

___

9. ἐδίωκόν σε οἱ δοῦλοι.

___

10. ἡμᾶς πέμπει ἡ βασίλισσα.

___

Exercise 16-F: Transform the sentences with passive verbs into sentences of equivalent meaning but with active verbs. The procedure to be followed is indicated by the model.

Model: τὰ τέκνα ἐβαπτίζοντο ὑπὸ τοῦ ἀποστόλου.

Answer: ὁ ἀπόστολος ἐβάπτιζεν τὰ τέκνα.

1. ὑμεῖς ἐδιώκεσθε ὑπ' ἐμοῦ.

____

2. αὐτὴ ἤγετο ὑπὸ τῶν προφητῶν.

____

3. ἐγὼ θεραπεύομαι ὑπὸ τοῦ κυρίου.

____

4. ὁ λόγος ἐκηρύσσετο ὑφ' ἡμῶν.

____

5. ἡ φωνὴ τοῦ κυρίου ἠκούετο ὑπὸ τῶν μαθητῶν αὐτοῦ.

____

6. οἱ ἀπόστολοι διδάσκονται ὑπὸ τοῦ Ἰησοῦ.

____

7. ὁ καλὸς δοῦλος ἐλύετο ὑπὸ τῶν ἀδελφῶν.

____

8. δοξάζεται ἡ ἐκκλησία ὑπὸ τῆς χήρας.

____

9. ἡ ἄμπελος ἐφυτεύετο ὑπὸ σοῦ.

____

10. οἱ οἶκοι ἑτοιμάζονται ὑφ' ὑμῶν.

____

Exercises to Lesson Seventeen

Exercise 17-A: Give the aorist active, middle, and passive forms corresponding to each of the following present active forms (i.e., retain the person and number of the given form, as in the model supplied.

All of the verbs in this exercise are regular in the tenses involved, though some phonological modification of consonant stems is necessary (see Pars. 93f, 126f).

Present Active	Aorist Active	Aorist Middle	Aorist Passive
Model: λύομεν	ἐλύσαμεν	ἐλυσάμεθα	ἐλύθημεν
1. πιστεύεις			
2. βαπτίζει			
3. δοξάζετε			
4. πέμπουσιν			
5. ἄρχω			
6. διώκομεν			

Exercise 17-B: Fill in the blank spaces in the table below with the missing forms:

Present Active	Aorist Active	Aorist Middle	Aorist Passive
1.		ἐλούσασθε	
2. πειράζετε			
3.	ἐβούλευσαν		
4. διώκουσιν			
5.			ἐπιστεύθησαν
6. ἄρχομεν			

Exercise 17-C: Put an X in each appropriate space below; imitate the model:

	Person 1	Person 2	Person 3	Number Sg.	Number Pl.	Pr	Impf.	Fut.	Aor.	Act.	Mid.	Pas.
Model: λύετε		X			X	X				X		
1. πιστεύσεις												
2. ἠλπίσθητε												
3. ἔγραψαν												
4. ἐβαπτισάμην												
5. ἔστρεφεν												
6. ἤχθησαν												
7. δοξάζουσιν												
8. ἡτοιμάσαμεν												
9. θεραπεύει												
10. ἐλίποντο (from λείπω)												
11. βουλεύσομεν												
12. ἔσωσα												
13. πειράσετε												
14. ἐτάχθης												
15. ἐκάλυπτεν												

Exercise 17-D: Transform the sentences with active verbs into sentences of equivalent meaning with passive verbs. Retain the tense of the verb in the given sentence, but adjust the person and number if necessary (see Exercise 16-E for model).

1. οἱ μαθηταὶ ἐβάπτισαν τὰ τέκνα.

____

2. ὁ ἀπόστολος ἔπεμψέν με.

____

3. ἐδιώξατε ὑμεῖς τοὺς προφήτας.

____

4. ἡμεῖς ἡτοιμάσαμεν τὰς ἐκκλησίας.

____

5. νόμους ἔγραψαν οἱ ἄνθρωποι.

____

6. ἐγὼ ἤκουσα τὰς φωνὰς αὐτῶν.

____

7. ἔσωσεν ὁ κύριος τοὺς δούλους αὐτοῦ.

____

8. ὁ Παῦλος ἐκήρυξεν τὸ εὐαγγέλιον.

____

9. αὐτοὶ ἐδόξασάν σε.

____

10. οὗτος ὁ στρατιώτης ἐπείρασεν ὑμᾶς.

____

<u>Exercise 17-E</u>: Write, on the line provided at the right, the form of λούω, <u>bathe</u>, which correctly translates the verb in the sentence before it:

<u>Model</u>: I am bathing. λούομαι

1. The children are bathing. ____________
2. The children are being bathed by their sister. ____________
3. We were bathing. (Impf.) ____________
4. We bathed. (Aorist) ____________
5. We were bathing the children. (Impf.) ____________
6. We bathed the children. (Aorist) ____________
7. We were being bathed by our sister. (Impf.) ____________
8. We were bathed by our sister. (Aorist) ____________
9. We have bathed. (Aorist) ____________
10. The children let themselves be bathed. (Aor.) ____________

Exercises to Lesson Eighteen

Exercise 18-A: Transform the sentences with active verbs into equivalent sentences with passive verbs. Retain the tense of the verb in the given sentence, but adjust the person and number if necessary. (For a model, see Exercise 16-E).

1. τὸν δοῦλον τὸν πιστὸν λύσει ὁ κύριος.

____

2. οἱ ἀπόστολοι πέμψουσιν ἡμᾶς.

____

3. ἡ ἐκκλησία ἀκούσει με. (See Par. 128)

____

4. ὁ θεὸς σώσει ὑμᾶς. (See Par. 128)

____

5. τὰς ἐντολὰς γράψουσιν οἱ προφῆται. (See Par. 130)

____

6. οἱ στρατιῶται ἐκεῖνοι διώξουσίν σε.

____

7. ὁ κύριος ἄξει τὴν ἐκκλησίαν αὐτοῦ.

____

8. ὁ Ἰησοῦς τὸν τυφλὸν θεραπεύσει.

____

9. ὁ Ἰωάννης ἑτοιμάσει τὴν ὁδὸν τοῦ κυρίου.

____

10. ὁ μαθητὴς βαπτίσει τοὺς ἁμαρτωλοὺς τούτους.

____

Exercise 18-B: Write, in the space provided at the right, the correct form of the verb λούω, bathe, which translates the verb in the sentence which precedes it:

Model: They will bathe. λούσονται

1. She will bathe the child. ____________
2. The child will bathe. ____________
3. The children will be bathed. ____________
4. She had the child bathed. (Aor.) ____________
5. She will have the child bathed. ____________
6. They were bathing the children. ____________
7. The children were bathing. ____________
8. The child was being bathed. ____________
9. You (sg.) will bathe. ____________
10. You (pl.) will be bathed. ____________
11. We shall bathe. ____________
12. I bathed. ____________
13. I had the children bathed. (Aor.) ____________
14. I shall have the children bathed. ____________
15. We shall be bathed. ____________

<u>Exercise 18-C</u>: Translate the English sentences on pages W 81 and W 82 into Greek. The verbs involved are those of Pars. 137-140. Imitate the models given below:

<u>Model</u> (a) I am becoming a disciple.
ἐγὼ γίνομαι μαθητής.

(b) I am coming.
ἐγὼ ἔρχομαι.

(c) The apostle is going.
ὁ ἀπόστολος πορεύεται.

(d) The prophet receives the word of the Lord.
ὁ προφήτης δέχεται τὸν λόγον τοῦ κυρίου.

(e) The man is taking the bread.
ὁ ἄνθρωπος λαμβάνει τὸν ἄρτον.

(f) The disciple is learning the commandments of God.
ὁ μαθητὴς μανθάνει τὰς ἐντολὰς τοῦ θεοῦ.

(g) The slave is eating bread.
ἄρτον ἐσθίει ὁ δοῦλος.

(h) The disciple is an apostle.
ὁ μαθητὴς ἀπόστολός ἐστιν.

(Exercise 18-C: See directions and model sentences on page W 79.)

1. We are becoming disciples.

2. We shall become disciples.

3. The disciple will become an apostle.

4. We shall come.

5. The apostles were going.

6. The disciple was coming.

7. The disciple has come.

8. The apostle has gone.

9. The apostle will go.

10. The apostle was going.

11. The prophet has received the word of the Lord.

12. The prophet will receive the word of the Lord.

13. The man was taking the bread.

14. The bread was taken (Aorist) by the man.

15. The man has taken the bread.

16. The man will take the bread.

17. The bread was being taken by the man.

18. The bread will be taken by the man.

19. The disciple will learn the commandments of God.

20. The disciple has learned the commandments of God.

21. The disciple was learning the commandments of God.

22. The slave was eating bread.

23. The slave has eaten bread.

24. The slave will eat bread.

25. The disciple was an apostle.

26. The disciple will be an apostle.

27. The disciples are apostles.

28. The disciples were apostles.

29. The disciples will be apostles.

30. We shall be disciples.

31. You (pl.) were slaves.

32. You will be a prophet.

33. We were disciples.

Exercises to Lesson Nineteen

Exercise 19-A: Indicate, by writing T or F in the ( ) provided, whether the statements below are true or false:

1. All first and second declension nouns with nom. sg. suffix ς also have gen. sg. suffix ου. ( )
2. All first and second declension nouns with gen. sg. suffix ου also have nom. sg. suffix ς. ( )
3. All nouns with acc. pl. suffix ους also have gen. sg. suffix ου. ( )
4. All nouns with gen. sg. suffix ου also have acc. pl. suffix ους. ( )
5. Some first declension nouns are feminine. ( )
6. Some first declension nouns are masculine. ( )
7. Some first declension nouns are neuter. ( )
8. Some second declension nouns are masculine. ( )
9. Some second declension nouns are feminine. ( )
10. Some second declension nouns are neuter. ( )
11. For neuter nouns, the nom. sg. suffix is the same as the acc. sg. suffix. ( )
12. For neuter nouns, the nom. pl. suffix is the same as the acc. pl. suffix. ( )
13. All first declension nouns with the nom. sg. suffix # are feminine. ( )
14. All first and second declension nouns with the nom. sg. suffix ς are masculine. ( )

15. All second declension nouns with the nom. sg. suffix ν are neuter. ( )

16. Some second declension nouns have the nom. sg. suffix #. ( )

<u>Exercise 19-B</u>: Fill in the blanks in the paradigms below. Do not use a lexicon.

	1.		2.		3.
Sg.N.	πλάνη	Sg.N.	σοφία	Sg.N.	θύρα
G.	____	G.	____	G.	____
D.	____	D.	____	D.	____
A.	____	A.	____	A.	____
Pl.N.	____	Pl.N.	____	Pl.N.	____
G.	____	G.	____	G.	____
D.	____	D.	____	D.	____
A.	____	A.	____	A.	____

	4.		5.		6.
Sg.N.	____	Sg.N.	θύελλα	Sg.N.	ᾅδης
G.	γενεᾶς	G.	____	G.	____
D.	____	D.	____	D.	____
A.	____	A.	____	A.	____
Pl.N.	____	Pl.N.	____	Pl.N.	____
G.	____	G.	____	G.	____
D.	____	D.	____	D.	____
A.	____	A.	____	A.	____

7. Sg.N. __________
G. ἀρχῆς
D. __________
A. ἀρχήν

Pl.N. __________
G. __________
D. __________
A. __________

8. Sg.N. __________
G. κλέπτου
D. __________
A. κλέπτην

Pl. N. __________
G. __________
D. __________
A. __________

9. Sg.N. __________
G. πρύμνης
D. __________
A. πρύμναν

Pl.N. __________
G. __________
D. __________
A. __________

10.Sg.N. πάροδος
G. __________
D. __________
A. __________

Pl.N. __________
G. __________
D. __________
A. __________

11.Sg.N. __________
G. __________
D. __________
A. __________

Pl.N. παρθένοι
G. __________
D. __________
A. __________

12.Sg.N. __________
G. πατρολῴου
D. __________
A. πατρολῴαν

Pl.N. __________
G. __________
D. __________
A. __________

13.Sg.N. __________
G. __________
D. __________
A. __________

Pl. N. __________
G. __________
D. __________
A. λιμούς

14.Sg. N. μαρτυρία
G. __________
D. __________
A. __________

Pl. N. __________
G. __________
D. __________
A. __________

15.Sg.N. __________
G. __________
D. __________
A. __________

Pl.N. μαρτύρια
G. __________
D. __________
A. __________

16.Sg.N.	______	17.Sg.N.	______	18.Sg.N.	λίτρα
G.	______	G.	______	G.	______
D.	______	D.	______	D.	______
A.	______	A.	______	A.	______
Pl.N.	λουτρά	Pl.N.	______	Pl.N.	______
G.	______	G.	______	G.	______
D.	______	D.	______	D.	______
A.	______	A.	λύτρα	A.	______

Exercises to Lesson Twenty

Exercise 20-A: Fill in the blanks in the paradigms below. Do not use a lexicon.

1.		2.		3.	
Sg.N.	ὁ ________	Sg.N.	________	Sg.N.	________
G.	τοῦ σκόλοπος	G.	________	G.	τοῦ παιδός
D.	________	D.	τῷ φύλακι	D.	________
A.	________	A.	τὸν ________	A.	________
Pl.N.	________	Pl. N.	________	Pl. N.	οἱ ________
G.	________	G.	________	G.	________
D.	________	D.	________	D.	________
A.	________	A.	________	A.	________

4.		5.		6.	
Sg.N.	________	Sg.N.	τὸ πνεῦμα	Sg.N.	________
G.	________	G.	________	G.	________
D.	________	D.	________	D.	________
A.	τὴν ἁγιότητα	A.	________	A.	________
Pl.N.	________	Pl.N.	________	Pl.N.	αἱ σάλπιγγες
G.	________	G.	________	G.	________
D.	________	D.	________	D.	________
A.	________	A.	________	A.	________

Exercise 20-B: In each of the sentences below, underline the subject and doubly underline the object:

1. ὁ ὑποκριτὴς διυλίζει τὸν κώνωπα.

2. τρώγει σάρκα ἡ ἀλώπηξ.

3. μάστιγας εἶχον βασανισταί.

4. ὄρνις τὰ νόσσια ἐπισυνάγει.

5. ἐπισυνάγει ὄρνιξ τὴν νοσσιάν.

6. σφραγίδα ἄγγελος ἤνοιξεν.

The following Vocabulary may be used in connection with Exercise 20-C.

Adjectives		Nouns	
ἀγαπητός, ή, όν,	beloved	ἀλώπηξ, ἀλώπεκος, ἡ,	fox
ἅγιος, α, ον,	holy	Ἄραψ, Ἄραβος, ὁ,	Arab
αἰώνιος, ον,	eternal	μώλωψ, μώλωπος, ὁ,	bruise
δίκαιος, α, ον,	just	ὄνομα, -ματος, τό,	name
μακάριος, α, ον,	blessed	παῖς, παιδός, ὁ	servant, child, boy
νεκρός, ά, όν,	dead	πνεῦμα, -ματος, τό,	spirit
τυφλός, ή, όν,	blind	σάρξ, σαρκός, ἡ,	flesh
Other		σφραγίς, -ῖδος, ἡ,	seal
αὐτός, ή, ό,	see Lesson 14.	φλόξ, φλογός, ἡ,	flame
οὗτος, αὕτη, τοῦτο,	see Lesson 14.	φύλαξ, φύλακος, ὁ,	watchman
ἐκεῖνος, η, ο,	see Lesson 14.	φῶς, φωτός, τό,	light

Exercise 20-C: Put an X in the ( ) before the Greek expressions which correctly render the English expressions which precede them.

1. Blessed is the name.
( ) τὸ ὄνομα τὸ μακάρια
( ) μακάριον τὸ ὄνομα
( ) τὸ ὄνομα τὸ μακάριον

2. The holy Spirit.
( ) πνεῦμα ἡ ἁγία
( ) τὸ ἅγιον πνεῦμα
( ) τὸ πνεῦμα ἅγιον

3. The beloved servant.
( ) ὁ ἀγαπητὸς παιδός
( ) ἀγαπητὸς ὁ παῖς
( ) ὁ παῖς ὁ ἀγαπητός

4. The light is eternal.
( ) αἰώνιον τὸ φῶς
( ) τὸ φῶς τὸ αἰώνιον
( ) τὸ φῶς αἰώνιος

5. The watchman is blind.
( ) ὁ τυφλὸς φύλαξ
( ) ὁ φύλαξ ὁ τυφλός
( ) ὁ φύλαξ τυφλός

6. The dead foxes.
( ) νεκραὶ αἱ ἀλώπεκες
( ) αἱ νεκραὶ ἀλώπεκες
( ) αἱ ἀλώπεκες νεκραί

7. The Arabs are just.
( ) δίκαιοι οἱ Ἄραβοι
( ) οἱ Ἄραβες δίκαιοι
( ) οἱ δίκαιοι Ἄραβες

8. The light of the flame.
( ) τὸ τῆς φλογὸς φῶς
( ) ἡ τοῦ φλογὸς φῶς
( ) ἡ φῶς τοῦ φλογός

9. The eternal flame.
( ) ἡ φλὸξ αἰωνία
( ) αἰώνιος ἡ φλόξ
( ) ἡ φλὸξ ἡ αἰώνιος

10. The seal of the Spirit.
( ) τὸ πνεῦμα τῆς σφραγῖδος
( ) ἡ σφραγὶς τοῦ πνεύματος
( ) τὸ τῆς σφραγῖδος πνεῦμα

11. The bruises of the flesh.

( ) οἱ μώλωποι τῆς σαρκῆς
( ) οἱ μώλωπες τῆς σαρκοῦ
( ) οἱ μώλωπες οἱ τῆς σαρκός

12. The same Spirit.

( ) αὐτὴ τὸ πνεῦμα
( ) τὸ αὐτὸ πνεῦμα
( ) τὸ πνεῦμα αὐτό.

13. Those servants.

( ) οἱ ἐκεῖνοι παῖδες
( ) οἱ παῖδες ἐκεῖνοι
( ) οἱ παῖδες ἐκεῖναι

14. This flesh.

( ) ἡ σὰρξ αὗτη
( ) ἡ σὰρξ ταῦτα
( ) ταύτη ἡ σάρξ

<u>Exercise 20-D</u>: Fill in the blank spaces in the Greek sentences so that they will correctly translate the English sentences which precede them. Make use of the Vocabulary in the preceding Exercise 20-C, if necessary.

1. The Word became flesh.
   ὁ λόγος ____________ ἐγένετο.
2. Paul received a thorn for the flesh.
   Παῦλος ἐδέξατο σκόλοπα ____________
3. The Lord gave us his flesh.
   ὁ κύριος ἔδωκεν ἡμῖν ________________ αὐτοῦ.
4. The works of the flesh are evil.
   πονηρὰ τὰ ἔργα _________________
5. These are the names of the disciples.
   ταῦτά εἰσιν τὰ τῶν μαθητῶν _________________
6. The disciples are faithful to the name of the Lord.
   οἱ μαθηταὶ πιστοὶ ____________________ τοῦ κυρίου.
7. The name of the Lord is holy.
   ἅγιον _________________ τὸ τοῦ κυρίου.
8. The glory of his name is manifest.
   φανερὰ ἡ δόξα _________________ αὐτοῦ.
9. We shall receive the seal of the Spirit.
   δεξόμεθα τὴν σφραγῖδα __________________
10. We shall receive the Spirit of grace.
    δεξόμεθα _________________ τῆς χάριτος.
11. The watchman sees the Arabs.
    ὁ φύλαξ ___________________ βλέπει.

12. The Arabs see the watchman.

τὸν φύλακα ______________ βλέπουσιν.

13. The Arab is dead.

νεκρὸς ________________

14. The servant of the Arab is dead.

νεκρὸς ὁ παῖς ____________________

15. The servants are faithful to the Arabs.

οἱ παῖδες πιστοὶ __________________

16. Jesus healed the boy.

ἐθεράπευσεν ὁ Ἰησοῦς ______________

17. The boy was healed by Jesus.

ἐθεραπεύθη ὑπὸ τοῦ Ἰησοῦ __________

18. Jesus healed the boy's bruises.

ἐθεράπευσεν ὁ Ἰησοῦς τοὺς μώλωπας _______________

19. The boys have a fox.

ἔχουσιν ἀλώπεκα _________________

20. The watchman gave the fox to the boys.

ἔδωκεν ὁ φύλαξ τὴν ἀλώπεκα _______________

21. the boy gave the fox to the watchman.

ἔδωκεν ὁ παῖς τὴν ἀλώπεκα ________________

22. The boys' fox is dead.

νεκρὰ ἡ ἀλώπηξ __________________

23. The watchman's fox is dead.

νεκρὰ ἡ ἀλώπηξ __________________

24. The spirits of the righteous are blessed.

________________ τῶν δικαίων μακάρια.

25. The Lord knows the names of the righteous spirits.
οἶδεν ὁ κύριος τὰ ὀνόματα ________________ τῶν δικαίων.

26. The Lord will send his holy Spirit.
πέμψει ὁ κύριος ________________ αὐτοῦ τὸ ἅγιον.

27. The servants of the Lord are the lights of the world.
οἱ παῖδες τοῦ κυρίου εἰσὶν τὰ ____________ τὰ τοῦ κόσμου.

28. The Lord will send the Spirit of light.
πέμψει ὁ κύριος τὸ πνεῦμα τὸ ________________

29. The servant sees the light of the Spirit.
βλέπει ὁ παῖς τὸ ________________ τὸ τοῦ πνεύματος.

30. The servants are watchmen.
________________ εἰσιν οἱ παῖδες.

31. The woman was made well (=was saved) from that hour.
ἐσώθη ________________ ἀπὸ τῆς ὥρας ἐκείνης.

32. He washed their feet.
ἔνιψεν ________________ αὐτῶν.

33. I have baptized you with water.
ἐβάπτισα ὑμᾶς ________________ (Use dative.)

34. The son of this woman is dead.
νεκρὸς ὁ υἱὸς ________________ ταύτης.

35. He gave these things to the women.
ταῦτα ἔδωκεν ________________

36. We hear the voices of the women.
ἀκούομεν τὰς φωνὰς ________________

Exercises to Lesson Twenty-One

Exercise 21-A: Fill in the blank spaces in the paradigms:

1. Sg.N. ______
G. τοῦ χαρακτῆρος
D. ______
A. ______

Pl.N. ______
G. ______
D. ______
A. ______

2. Sg.N. ______
G. ______
D. τῷ ἀγῶνι
A. ______

Pl.N. ______
G. ______
D. ______
A. ______

3. Sg.N. ______
G. ______
D. ______
A. τὸν λιμένα

Pl.N. ______
G. ______
D. ______
A. ______

4. Sg.N. ______
G. ______
D. ______
A. ______

Pl.N. οἱ παντοκράτορες
G. ______
D. ______
A. ______

5. Sg.N. ______
G. ______
D. τῷ κανόνι
A. ______

Pl.N. ______
G. ______
D. ______
A. ______

6. Sg.N. ______
G. ______
D. ______
A. ______

Pl.N. ______
G. ______
D. ______
A. τοὺς δράκοντας

7. Sg.N. ὁ ποιμὴν ὁ καλός
G. ______
D. ______
A. ______
Pl.N. ______

8. Sg.N. ὁ ἄφρων μαθητής
G. ______
D. ____ ἄφρονι ______
A. ______
Pl.N. ______

G. ____________________ G. ____________________

D. ____________________ D. ____________________

A. ____________________ A. ____________________

<u>Exercise 21-B</u>: Fill in the blanks so that the Greek sentences will correctly translate the English sentences which precede them. Use the Vocabulary of Lesson Twenty-One.

1. I am the good shepherd.
   ἐγώ εἰμι ____________________ ὁ καλός.

2. I shall smite the shepherd.
   πατάξω ____________________

3. The sheep of the shepherd are foolish.
   ἄφρονα τὰ πρόβατα ____________________

4. The disciple gave bread to his mother.
   ἔδωκεν ὁ μαθητὴς ἄρτον ________________ αὐτοῦ.

5. This mother bore male children.
   αὕτη ἡ μήτηρ ἔτεκεν τέκνα ____________

6. I am a debtor to Greeks.
   ____________________ ὀφειλέτης εἰμί.

7. The Greeks are teaching the apostles.
   τοὺς ἀποστόλους διδάσκουσιν ________________

8. The apostles are teaching the Greeks.
   οἱ ἀπόστολοι διδάσκουσιν ____________________

9. Nicodemus was a ruler of the Jews.
   Νικόδημος ἦν ________________ τῶν 'Ιουδαίων.

10. The soldiers of the leader pursued Jesus.
    ἐδίωξαν τὸν 'Ιησοῦν οἱ στρατιῶται ________________

11. A man planted a vineyard.
    ______________ ἄνθρωπος ἐφύτευσεν.

12. They have stopped lions' mouths.
    ἔφραξαν στόματα ______________

13. This is the saviour of the world.
    οὗτός ἐστιν ____________ τοῦ κόσμου.

14. The sons of this age are evil.
    πονηροὶ οἱ υἱοὶ τούτου ________________

15. Jesus healed the daughter of the rich man.
    ὁ Ἰησοῦς ἐθεράπευσεν ________________ τοῦ πλούτου.

16. We sent messengers to the men.
    ἡμεῖς ἐπέμψαμεν ἀγγέλους ______________ (Use ἀνήρ)

17. The prophet was baptizing the men.
    ἐβάπτιζεν ὁ προφήτης ________________ (Use ἀνήρ)

18. The father sent the son.
    ἔπεμψεν τὸν υἱὸν ______________

19. The Lord is greater than the demons.
    ὁ κύριος μείζων ________________

20. Paul baptized more Greeks than Jews.
    ὁ Παῦλος ἐβάπτισεν ____________ Ἕλληνας ἢ Ἰουδαίους.

21. More Greeks than Jews heard Paul.
    Παῦλον ἤκουσαν ______________ Ἕλληνες ἢ Ἰουδαῖοι.

22. The children are smaller than their father.
    τὰ τέκνα ______________ τοῦ πατρὸς αὐτῶν.

23. The Son of God is better than the angels.
    ____________ τῶν ἀγγέλων ἐστὶν ὁ τοῦ θεοῦ υἱός.

24. The angels are better than these men.

______________ τούτων τῶν ἀνδρῶν εἰσιν οἱ ἄγγελοι.

25. The disciples are sober men.

______________ ἄνδρες εἰσὶν οἱ μαθηταί.

26. The evil one is the ruler of the power of the air.

ὁ πονηρός ἐστιν ὁ ἄρχων τῆς ἐξουσίας ______________

27. The son was sent by the father.

ὁ υἱὸς ἐπέμφθη ὑπὸ ______________

28. The apostles were taught by the Greeks.

οἱ ἀπόστολοι ἐδιδάχθησαν ὑπὸ ______________

29. The soldiers were sent by their leaders.

οἱ στρατιῶται ἐπέμφθησαν ὑπὸ ______________

30. You sent a slave to the daughters of the ruler.

ὑμεῖς ἐπέμψατε δοῦλον ______________ τοῦ ἡγεμόνος.

31. She wiped his feet with her hair (dat. pl.). (Supply articles.)

ἐξέμαξεν ______________ αὐτῆς______________ αὐτοῦ.

32. There will be weeping and gnashing of teeth. (Supply the article.)

ἐκεῖ ἔσται ὁ κλαυθμὸς καὶ ὁ βρυγμὸς ______________

33. I, Paul, have written with my own hand. (Do not translate "own".)

ἐγὼ Παῦλος ἔγραψα τῇ ἐμῇ ______________

34. He works with his hands. (dat.)

ἐργάζεται ______________ αὐτοῦ.

35. He will baptize you with fire. (dat.)

αὐτὸς ὑμᾶς βαπτίσει ______________

36. He gave holy things to the dogs.

ἔδωκεν τὰ ἅγια ______________

Exercises to Lesson Twenty-Two

Exercise 22-A: Complete the paradigms below:

1. Sg.N. ὁ βαθὺς ὕπνος
   G. ____
   D. ____
   A. ____

   Pl.N. ____
   G. ____
   D. ____
   A. ____

2. Sg.N. τὸ βαρὺ φορτίον
   G. ____
   D. ____
   A. ____

   Pl.N. ____
   G. ____
   D. ____
   A. ____

3. Sg.N. ἡ βραδεῖα γλῶσσα
   G. ____
   D. ____
   A. ____

   Pl.N. ____
   G. ____
   D. ____
   A. ____

4. Sg.N. ὁ γλυκὺς βότρυς
   G. ____
   D. ____
   A. ____

   Pl.N. ____
   G. ____
   D. ____
   A. ____

5. Sg.N. ὁ τραχὺς τόπος
   G. ____
   D. ____
   A. ____

   Pl.N. ____

6. Sg.N. ὁ πραῢς ἀνήρ
   G. ____
   D. ____
   A. ____

   Pl.N. ____

G. ____________________ G. ____________________

D. ____________________ D. ____________________

A. ____________________ A. ____________________

Exercise 22-B: Put an X in the ( ) before the Greek expression which correctly renders the English:

1. Hades is deep.
( ) βαθεῖα ὁ ᾅδης
( ) βαθὺς ὁ ᾅδης
( ) βαθὺ ὁ ᾅδης
( ) ὁ βαθὺς ᾅδης

2. Blessed are the meek.
( ) μακάριοι οἱ πραεῖς
( ) οἱ μακάριοι πραεῖς
( ) μακάριος ὁ πραΰς
( ) ὁ πραΰς ὁ μακάριος

3. My yoke is heavy.
( ) ὁ ζυγός μου ἐστιν βαρύος
( ) ὁ βαρύς μου ζυγός
( ) βαρὺς ὁ ζυγός μου
( ) ὁ ζυγός μου ὁ βαρύς

4. The female child.
( ) τὸ τέκνον θῆλυ
( ) τὸ θήλεια τέκνον
( ) θῆλυ τὸ τέκνον
( ) τὸ τέκνον τὸ θῆλυ

5. The straight way.
( ) εὐθὺς ἡ ὁδός
( ) ἡ ὁδὸς εὐθεῖα
( ) ἡ εὐθεῖα ὁδός
( ) ἡ εὐθὺς ὁδός

6. The earth is broad.
( ) πλατὺς ἡ γῆ
( ) πλατεῖα ἡ γῆ
( ) ἡ γῆ πλατύς
( ) ἡ γῆ ἡ πλατεῖα

7. The same sow.

( ) αὐτὴ ἡ ὗς
( ) ἡ ὗς αὐτή
( ) ἡ αὐτὴ ὗς
( ) ἡ αὐτῆς ὗς

8. They ate ears of corn.

( ) ἤσθιον στάχεις
( ) ἤσθιον στάχυους
( ) ἤσθιον στάχυας
( ) στάχυας ἤσθιεν

9. He gave him a fish.

( ) ἔδωκεν αὐτῷ ἰχθύν
( ) ἔδωκεν αὐτὸν ἰχθύι
( ) ἔδωκεν αὐτὸν ἰχθύς
( ) ἔδωκεν αὐτῷ ἰχθύας

10. The strength of the man.

( ) ὁ ἰσχὺς τοῦ ἀνδρός
( ) ὁ ἰσχὺς ὁ τοῦ ἀνδρός
( ) ἡ ἰσχὺς ἡ τῆς ἀνδρός
( ) ἡ ἰσχὺς ἡ τοῦ ἀνδρός

Exercise 22-C: Complete the paradigms below:

1. The strict sect

Sg.N. ἡ ἀκριβὴς αἵρεσις
G. ____________
D. ____________
A. ____________

Pl.N. ____________
G. ____________
D. ____________
A. ____________

2. The new creation

Sg.N. ἡ καινὴ κτίσις
G. ____________
D. ____________
A. ____________

Pl.N. ____________
G. ____________
D. ____________
A. ____________

3. The faithful priest

Sg.N. ὁ πιστὸς ἱερεύς

G. ______________________

D. ______________________

A. ______________________

Pl.N. ______________________

G. ______________________

D. ______________________

A. ______________________

4. The only son

Sg.N. ὁ μονογενὴς υἱός

G. ______________________

D. ______________________

A. ______________________

Pl.N. ______________________

G. ______________________

D. ______________________

A. ______________________

5. The false knowledge

Sg.N. ἡ ψευδὴς γνῶσις

G. ______________________

D. ______________________

A. ______________________

Pl.N. ______________________

G. ______________________

D. ______________________

A. ______________________

6. The weak vessel

Sg.N. τὸ ἀσθενὲς σκεῦος

G. ______________________

D. ______________________

A. ______________________

Pl. N. ______________________

G. ______________________

D. ______________________

A. ______________________

Exercise 22-D: Fill in the blanks so that the Greek will translate the English. Use the lists of words in Lesson 22.

1. We have a firm anchor of the soul.
   ἄγκυραν ἔχομεν τῆς ψυχῆς ________________

2. The word of God is effective.
   ὁ λόγος τοῦ θεοῦ ________________

3. Lucius was a kinsman of Paul.
   Λούκιος ἦν Παύλου ________________

4. The man became healthy.
   ἐγένετο ________________ ὁ ἄνθρωπος.

5. The child became healthy.
   ἐγένετο ________________ τὸ τέκνον.

6. The Pharisees sent the scribes.
   ἔπεμψαν οἱ Φαρισαῖοι ________________________

7. The scribes sent the Pharisees.
   ἔπεμψαν τοὺς Φαρισαίους ______________________

8. The Son of Man shall receive power.
   ὁ υἱὸς τοῦ ἀνθρώπου ________________ δέξεται.

9. This is the hope of our calling.
   αὕτη ἐστὶν ἡ ἐλπὶς ____________________ ἡμῶν.

10. We used to teach the traditions of the scribes.
    ἐδιδάσκομεν ______________________ τῶν γραμματέων.

11. The traditions of the scribes were being taught by us.
    ἐδιδάσκοντο _____________________ τῶν γραμματέων ὑφ' ἡμῶν.

12. Your bodies are members of Christ.
    τὰ σώματα ὑμῶν ________________ Χριστοῦ εἰσιν.

13. Love covers a multitude of sins.
    ἀγάπη καλυπτει ____________ ἁμαρτιῶν.

14. John was the son of pious parents.
    ὁ 'Ιωάννης ἦν ὁ υἱὸς ________________________________

Exercises to Lesson Twenty-Three

Exercise 23-A: Put an X in each of the appropriate spaces in the table below, imitating the model given.

	Person			Number		Pres.	Impf.	Act.	Mid.& Pass.
	1	2	3	Sg.	Pl.				
Model: ἀγαπῶ	X			X		X		X	
1. τιμώμεθα									
2. καλοῦμεν									
3. κρατεῖτε									
4. ζηλοῦσιν									
5. ἐζήτει									
6. ἐσταυροῦ									
7. ἐσταύρου									
8. ἠρώτα									
9. θεωρεῖσθε									
10. ἠρωτᾶτο									
11. ἐρωτᾶτε									
12. ἐφανεροῦντο									
13. λαλεῖ									
14. μαρτυροῦμαι									
15. πληροῦνται									
16. ἐτήρεις									
17. ἠρωτῶντο									
18. σταυροῖς									
19. ὁρῶσιν									
20. αἰτεῖται									

Exercise 23-B: Fill in the blank spaces in the table below with the missing forms, retaining the person and number of the given form:

Active		Middle and Passive	
Present	Imperfect	Present	Imperfect
1. δουλοῖς			
2.			ἐτιμῶντο
3.	ἐλαλεῖτε		
4.		ἀγαπώμεθα	
5. καλεῖ			
6.	ἐδήλου		
7.			ἐδηλοῦ
8.		ποιεῖται	
9. ἐρωτῶσιν			
10.	ἐνίκα		
11.		δικαιοῦσθε	
12.			ἐθεωρεῖτο
13.		πλανῶμαι	
14.		τηρῇ	
15. τιμᾷς			

Exercise 23-C: Supply the appropriate (contracted) form of the present active of ἀγαπάω.

1. ἐγώ σε ______________

2. ὁ θεὸς τὸν κόσμον ________________

3. σὺ τὴν μητέρα σου ________________

4. ἡμεῖς τοὺς ἀδελφοὺς ______________

5. ἡμᾶς οἱ ἀδελφοὶ __________________

Exercise 23-D: Supply the appropriate (contracted) form of the imperfect active of ἀγαπάω.

1. αὐτὴν ἐγὼ ____________________

2. ἡμεῖς τοὺς γονεῖς ἡμῶν __________________

3. ἡμᾶς οἱ γονεῖς ἡμῶν ____________________

4. τοὺς στρατιώτας ὁ ἡγεμὼν _________________

5. ὑμεῖς τὸν συγγενῆ μου ____________________

Exercise 23-E: Supply the appropriate (contracted) form of the present passive of ἀγαπάω.

1. ὁ κύριος ὑπὸ τῆς ἀδελφῆς ________________

2. ἡμεῖς ὑπ'αὐτῶν _____________________

3. οὗτοι ὑφ'ἡμῶν ______________________

4. ἐγὼ ὑπὸ τῶν ἀδελφῶν μου __________________

5. σὺ ὑπὸ τοῦ κυρίου ____________________

Exercise 23-F: Supply the appropriate (contracted) form of the imperfect passive of ἀγαπάω.

1. ἡ ἀδελφὴ ὑπὸ τοῦ ἀνδρὸς ________________

2. ἐγὼ ὑπὸ τοῦ πατρὸς ________________

3. ἐκεῖνοι ὑπὸ τῶν γονέων ________________

4. ἡμεῖς ὑπὸ τῶν τέκνων ἡμῶν ________________

5. ὑμεῖς υπὸ τοῦ υἱοῦ μου ________________

Exercise 23-G: Supply the appropriate (contracted)form of the present active of καλέω.

1. ὁ βασιλεὺς τὸν παῖδα αὐτοῦ ____________

2. ἐγὼ τὰ τέκνα μου ____________

3. ἡμεῖς ὑμᾶς ____________

4. ἡμᾶς ὑμεῖς ____________

5. ὁ συγγενής μου __________ με.

Exercise 23-H: Supply the appropriate (contracted) form of the imperfect active of καλέω.

1. ὁ ἐπιστάτης τὰς μαθητρίας ________________

2. σὺ τὸν πατέρα σου ________________

3. οἱ γονεῖς τοὺς υἱοὺς ________________

4. ἐγὼ τοὺς γονεῖς μου ________________

5. ἡμεῖς τὸν διδάσκαλον ________________

Exercise 23-I: Supply the appropriate (contracted) form of the present passive of καλέω.

1. οἱ μαθηταὶ ὑπὸ τοῦ κυρίου ____________________

2. ὁ τελώνης ὑπὸ τοῦ 'Ιησοῦ ____________________

3. ἡμεῖς ὑπὸ τοῦ βασιλέως ____________________

4. ὑμεῖς ὑπὸ τοῦ ἡγεμόνος ____________________

5. σὺ ὑπ' ἐμοῦ ______________

Exercise 23-J: Supply the appropriate (contracted) form of the imperfect passive of καλέω.

1. ὁ ἁλιεὺς ὑπὸ τοῦ αδελφοῦ αὐτοῦ ____________________

2. ἐγὼ ὑπὸ σοῦ ____________________

3. σὺ ὑφ' ἡμῶν ______________

4. τὰ πρόβατα ὑπὸ τοῦ ποιμένος ____________________

5. ἡμεῖς ὑπὸ τοῦ θεοῦ ____________________

Exercise 23-K: Supply the appropriate (contracted) form of the present active of σταυρόω.

1. ἐκεῖνοι τὸν κύριον τῆς δόξης ____________________

2. ὑμεῖς τὸν βασιλέα ἡμῶν ____________________

3. ἡμεῖς τοὺς μαθητὰς αὐτοῦ ____________________

4. ὁ στρατιώτης τὸν λῃστὴν ____________________

5. σὺ τὸν ἄνδρα ____________________

Exercise 23-L: Supply the appropriate (contracted) form of the imperfect active of σταυρόω.

1. οὗτοι τοὺς λῃστὰς ________________

2. ὁ βασανιστὴς δούλους ________________

3. σὺ τὸν υἱὸν τοῦ θεοῦ ______________

4. ἡμεῖς τοὺς φονεῖς ἐκείνους ______________

5. τὸν φονέα ἐγὼ _____________

Exercise 23-M: Supply the appropriate (contracted) form of the present passive of σταυρόω.

1. οἱ ἀδελφοὶ ἡμῶν ὑπὸ τῶν στρατιωτῶν ________________

2. ὁ φονεὺς ὑφ' ἡμῶν ________________

3. σὺ ὑπὸ βασανιστοῦ _______________

4. ἡμεῖς ὑπὸ τῶν ἐχθρῶν ἡμῶν ____________________

5. ὑμεῖς ὑπὸ τῶν ἀνδρῶν τῶν πονηρῶν __________________

Exercise 23-N: Supply the appropriate (contracted) form of the imperfect passive of σταυρόω.

1. οἱ δοῦλοι ὑπὸ βασανιστῶν ___________________

2. ὁ λῃστὴς ὑφ' ὑμῶν __________________

3. σὺ ὑπὸ τῶν ἐχθρῶν σου ________________

4. ἡμεῖς ὑπὸ τῶν στρατιωτῶν ___________________

5. ὑμεῖς ὑπὸ τῶν δούλων τοῦ βασιλέως __________________

<u>Exercise 23-0</u>: Transform the sentences from active to passive. Retain the tense of the verb, but alter the person and number if necessary. Imitate the model provided.

<u>Model</u>: ὁ πατὴρ ἀγαπᾷ τὸν υἱόν.
<u>Answer</u>: ὁ υἱὸς ἀγαπᾶται ὑπὸ τοῦ πατρός.

1. ἱλαρὸν δότην ἀγαπᾷ ὁ θεός.

    ____

2. ὁ ποιμὴν ὁ καλὸς ἀγαπᾷ τὰ πρόβατα.

    ____

3. ὁ πατὴρ ἡμῶν ἡμᾶς ἀγαπᾷ.

    ____

4. αἱ θυγατέρες μου ἀγαπῶσιν σε.

    ____

5. ὁ διδάσκαλος λαλεῖ λόγους παρακλήσεως.

    ____

6. σὺ λαλεῖς τὴν ἀλήθειαν.

    ____

7. ὁ κύριος φανεροῖ τὴν δόξαν αὐτοῦ.

    ____

8. ὑμεῖς τὸν σωτῆρα ἐσταυροῦτε.

    ____

9. οἱ Ἕλληνες ἡμᾶς ἐζήτουν.

    ____

10. ἡμεῖς ἠγαπῶμέν σε.

    ____

The Vocabulary below is to be used in connection with Exercise 23-P:

ἀγαπάω,	love	ἔργον, ου, τό,	work
ζητέω,	seek	θέλημα, θελήματος, τό,	will
λαλέω,	speak, tell	θεός, οῦ, ὁ,	God
πληρόω,	fill, fulfil	κόσμος, ου, ὁ,	world
ποιέω,	make, do	κύριος, ου, ὁ,	Lord
σταυρόω,	crucify	λόγος, ου, ὁ,	word
φανερόω,	manifest	μήτηρ, μητρός, ἡ,	mother
		πατήρ, πατρός, ὁ,	father
ἀλήθεια, ας, ἡ,	truth	προφήτης, ου, ὁ,	prophet
ἄνθρωπος, ου, ὁ,	man	σκότος, ους, τό,	darkness
γραφή, ῆς, ἡ,	scripture	στρατιώτης, ου, ὁ,	soldier
δόξα, ης, ἡ,	glory	σωτήρ, σωτῆρος, ὁ,	savior
ἐντολή, ῆς, ἡ,	commandment	χαρά, ᾶς, ἡ,	joy

Exercise 23-P: Making use of the Vocabulary on the preceding page, translate the following sentences into English:

1. ἀγαπήσεις τὸν θεόν σου.

____

2. ὁ πατήρ μου ἀγαπήσει αὐτόν.

____

3. ἠγάπησεν ὁ θεὸς τὸν κόσμον.

____

4. ἠγάπησαν οἱ ἄνθρωποι τὸ σκότος.

____

5. ἐποίησεν τὸ θέλημα τοῦ πατρός.

____

6. ποιῶ τὰ ἔργα τοῦ πατρός μου.

____

7. τὰς ἐντολὰς αὐτοῦ ποιοῦμεν.

____

8. ἐπληρώθη ὁ λόγος τοῦ προφήτου.

____

9. ἡ γραφὴ πληρωθήσεται.

____

10. ἡ χαρὰ ἡμῶν πληροῦται.

____

11. οἱ στρατιῶται ἐσταύρουν τὸν σωτῆρα τοῦ κόσμου.

____

12. ἐγὼ τὴν ἀλήθειαν λαλῶ.

____

13. ὁ κύριος ἐφανέρωσεν τὴν δόξαν αὐτοῦ.

____

14. ἡ μήτηρ σου ζητεῖ σε.

____

15. ὁ προφήτης λόγους ἀληθείας ἐλάλει.

____

16. ἡ ἀλήθεια τῶν λόγων ἡμῶν πληρωθήσεται.

____

17. ζητοῦμεν τὴν μητέρα τούτου τοῦ ἀνθρώπου.

____

18. οἱ προφῆται ἐλάλουν τὰς ἐντολάς τοῦ πατρὸς ἡμῶν.

____

19. ὁ κύριος τοῦ κόσμου τούτου ἔργα σκότους ἐποίησεν.

____

20. ὁ θεὸς ἐπλήρου τὴν χαρὰν τοῦ σωτῆρος.

____

Exercises to Lesson Twenty-Four

Exercise 24-A: Write in the blank space in each sentence the proper form of the noun or adjective given (in the nominative singular) in the parentheses at the left. (Imitate the model below.)

Model: (κύριος) καλοῦμεν 'Ιησοῦν κύριον.
We call Jesus Lord.

(βασιλεύς) 1. αὐτὸν καλήσομεν ____________ ἡμῶν.
We shall call him our king.

(βασιλεύς) 2. ἐκλήθη ____________ τῶν 'Ιουδαίων.
He was called king of the Jews.

(μακάριος) 3. κληθησόμεθα ____________
We shall be called blessed.

(πατήρ) 4. ὁ 'Ιησοῦς τὸν θεὸν ἐκάλεσεν __________ αὐτοῦ.
Jesus called God his father.

(ἄνθρωπος) 5. ἐδίδασκεν ὁ 'Ιησοῦς ____________
τὴν ὁδὸν τῆς ἀληθείας.
Jesus taught men the way of truth.

(ἄνθρωπος) 6. ἐγνώρισεν ὁ 'Ιησοῦς ____________
τὴν ὁδὸν τῆς ἀληθείας.
Jesus made the way of truth known to men.

(ἅγιος) 7. ἐκάλεσεν ὁ Παῦλος τὰς ἐντολὰς __________
Paul called the commandments holy.

(δίκαιος) 8. τὸν νόμον ἐκάλεσεν ________________

He called the law just.

(ἀληθής) 9. ἐκάλεσαν τοὺς λόγους τοῦ κυρίου ___________

They called the words of the Lord true.

(πονηρός) 10. τὰ ἔργα τῆς σαρκὸς ἐκάλεσεν _____________

He called the works of the flesh evil.

(γραμματεύς) 11. ἐδίδαξαν οἱ διδάσκαλοι τὸν νόμον __________

The teachers taught the law to scribes.

(γραμματεύς) 12. ἐγνώρισαν οἱ διδάσκαλοι τὸν νόμον _________

The teachers made the law known to scribes.

(γραμματεύς) 13. ἐπίστευσαν οἱ διδάσκαλοι τὸν νόμον ________

The teachers entrusted the law to scribes.

(σημεῖον) 14. ᾔτησαν οἱ 'Ιουδαῖοι ________________

The Jews asked for signs.

(σημεῖον) 15. ᾐτήσαντο οἱ Ἕλληνες _______________

The Greeks asked for signs.

(βασιλεύς) 16. ᾐτήσατο ἡ θυγάτηρ τῆς 'Ηρῳδιάδος __________

τὴν κεφαλὴν τοῦ 'Ιωάννου τοῦ βαπτιστοῦ.

The daughter of Herodias asked the king

(supply the article) for the head of John the Baptist.

(γραφή) 17. ὁ παῖς τὸν διδάσκαλον ἠρώτα _____ __________

The child asked the teacher about the scripture.

(Supply the article.)

(πατήρ) 18. ______________ ἔχομεν τὸν 'Αβραάμ.
We have Abraham for a father.

(ἐχθρός) 19. ἡγούμεθά σε ______________
We count you as an enemy.

(ἐχθρός) 20. ἡγούμεθά σε ὡς ______________
We count you as an enemy.

(ἐντολή) 21. ἐδιδάχθημεν ______________
We have been taught the commandments. (Supply the article.)

(ἐντολή) 22. ἐπιστεύθημεν ______________
We have been entrusted with the commandments. (Supply the article.)

(ἐντολή) 23. ἡμῖν ἐγνωρίσθησαν ______________
The commandments have been made known to us. (Supply the article.)

(προφήτης) 24. εἴχομεν τοὺς μαθητὰς ὡς ______________
We regarded the disciples as prophets.

(προφήτης) 25. εἴχομεν τοὺς μαθητὰς εἰς ______________
We regarded the disciples as prophets.

Exercises to Lesson Twenty-Five

Exercise 25-A: Fill in the blank with the appropriate preposition, so that the Greek will correctly render the English:

1. A man is coming into the city.
   ἄνθρωπος ἔρχεται _________ τὴν πόλιν..

2. He is coming instead of his brother.
   ἔρχεται ____________ τοῦ ἀδελφοῦ αὐτοῦ.

3. The brother is coming instead of his sister.
   ἔρχεται ὁ ἀδελφὸς ____________ τῆς ἀδελφῆς αὐτοῦ.

4. They were baptized with the Holy Spirit.
   ἐβαπτίσθησαν _________ τῷ πνεύματι τῷ ἁγίῳ.

5. They were baptized with their father.
   ἐβαπτίσθησαν _________ τῷ πατρὶ αὐτῶν.

6. The men are staying in the city.
   οἱ ἄνδρες μένουσιν _______ τῇ πόλει.

7. They confessed the Lord Jesus with their mouths.
   ὡμολόγησαν τὸν κύριον Ἰησοῦν __________ τοῖς στόμασιν αὐτῶν.

8. Jesus came for the forgiveness of sins.
   ὁ Ἰησοῦς ἔρχεται __________ ἄφεσιν ἁμαρτιῶν.

9. Jesus taught in the midst of his disciples.
   ὁ Ἰησοῦς ἐδίδασκεν _______________ τῶν μαθητῶν αὐτοῦ.

10. Jesus came after John the Baptist.
    ὁ Ἰησοῦς ἦλθεν _______ τοῦ Ἰωάννου τοῦ βαπτιστοῦ.

11. The men came without us.
    οἱ ἄνδρες ἦλθον ________ ἡμῶν.

12. The men received a denarius apiece.
    ἔλαβον οἱ ἄνδρες __________ δηνάριον.

13. The Father sent the Son into the world.
ὁ πατὴρ τὸν υἱὸν ἔπεμψεν ______ τὸν κόσμον.

14. The scribes taught the Law apart from the prophets.
οἱ γραμματεῖς τὸν νόμον ἐδίδασκον ________ τῶν προφητῶν.

15. The Pharisees loved the Law in place of the Gospel.
ἠγάπησαν οἱ Φαρισαῖοι τὸν νόμον _________ τοῦ εὐαγγελίου.

16. We shall have peace in those days.
ἕξομεν ἡμεῖς εἰρήνην _________ ταῖς ἡμέραις ἐκείναις.

17. The Lord will be with us.
ὁ κύριος ἔσται _______ ἡμῖν.

18. Jesus taught by means of parables.
ὁ Ἰησοῦς ἐδίδασκεν ________ παραβολαῖς.

19. The Holy Spirit will come after the Son.
τὸ πνεῦμα τὸ ἅγιον ἐλεύσεται __________ τοῦ υἱοῦ.

20. Jesus said these things in the cities.
ταῦτα ἔλεγεν ὁ Ἰησοῦς _______ ταῖς πόλεσιν.

21. We are in the Church of God.
_______ τῇ ἐκκλησίᾳ τοῦ θεοῦ ἐσμεν.

22. The men come with their fathers.
ἔρχονται οἱ ἄνδρες ________ τοῖς πατράσιν αὐτῶν.

23. We shall be saved by the word of truth.
σωθησόμεθα ________ τῷ λόγῳ τῆς ἀληθείας.

24. The Holy Spirit is with these men.
τὸ ἅγιον πνεῦμά ἐστιν _______ τούτοις τοῖς ἀνδράσιν.

25. The brothers came by twos. (=two by two)
οἱ ἀδελφοὶ ἦλθον _______ δύο.

26. We shall go into the house of the Lord.
ἐλευσόμεθα _________ τὸν οἶκον τοῦ κυρίου.

Exercise 25-B: A substantive expression (i.e., a noun, a pronoun, or a noun with its article and other modifiers) in the nominative case is given in parentheses after each Greek sentence below. Write the form of this expression which is permissible in the space provided. Imitate the model.

Model: ἄνθρωπος ἔρχεται ἐκ τῆς πόλεως. (ἡ πόλις)

1. οἱ μαθηταὶ πιστοὶ ἔσονται ἄχρι __________ (θάνατος)
2. ὁ Ἰησοῦς ἐδίδασκεν ταῦτα ἔμπροσθεν __________ (οἱ μαθηταί)
3. οἱ μαθηταὶ ἐδίδασκον ταῦτα ______ χάριν. (ἡμεῖς)
4. τας ἐντολὰς αὐτοῦ ἐτήρησαν ἕως __________ (αὕτη ἡ ἡμέρα)
5. ὡμολόγησα τὸν κύριον Ἰησοῦν ἐνώπιον ______ (σύ)
6. ὁ Ἰωάννης ἐδίδασκεν πρὸ __________ (ὁ Ἰησοῦς)
7. ὁ υἱὸς τοῦ θεοῦ ἐλεύσεται ἀπὸ __________ (οἱ οὐρανοί)
8. ὁ πατηρ τὸν υἱὸν ἔπεμψεν ἕνεκεν ________ (υμεῖς)
9. ταῦτα ἔλεγον ἔμπροσθεν __________ (ὁ βασιλεύς)
10. ὁ φύλαξ ἐστὶν πρὸ __________ (ἡ θύρα)
11. ἀπέθανεν ἕνεκα __________ (ἡ βασιλεία)
12. πιστεύομεν εἰς __________ (ὁ κύριος)
13. οὗτοι οἱ ἄνδρες εἰσὶν ἐξ ________ (αὐτός)
14. οἱ Ἰουδαῖοι σωθήσονται σὺν __________ (τὰ ἔθνη)
15. οἱ ἀπόστολοι ἐδίδασκον ἐν __________ (ἡ ἁπλότης, Gen. τῆς ἁπλότητος)

16. σκανδαλισθήσεσθε ἐν ἐμοὶ ἐν ____________ ταύτῃ. (ἡ νύξ, νυκτός)

17. ἔπεσα ἔμπροσθεν ________________ αὐτοῦ. (ὁ πούς, ποδός)

18. αὐτὸς ὑμᾶς βαπτίσει ἐν πνεύματι ἁγίῳ καὶ ________ (τὸ πῦρ, πυρός)

19. πολλάκις γὰρ πίπτει εἰς _____________ (τὸ πῦρ, πυρός)

20. πολλάκις γὰρ πίπτει εἰς _____________ (τὸ ὕδωρ, ὕδατος)

Exercises to Lesson Twenty-Six

Exercise 26-A: Fill in the blank with the appropriate preposition, so that the Greek will correctly render the English:

1. They will go through Judaea.
   πορεύσονται _______ τῆς Ἰουδαίας.
2. God made the world by his word.
   ὁ θεὸς τὸν κόσμον ἐποίησεν _______ τοῦ λόγου αὐτοῦ.
3. They are taking counsel against us.
   λαμβάνουσιν συμβούλιον ________ ἡμῶν.
4. The Son of Man will come with his angels.
   ἐλεύσεται ὁ υἱὸς τοῦ ἀνθρώπου _______ τῶν ἀγγέλων αὐτοῦ.
5. His sisters are with him.
   αἱ ἀδελφαὶ αὐτοῦ _________ αὐτόν εἰσιν.
6. Christ died for our sins according to the scriptures.
   Χριστὸς ἀπέθανεν ὑπὲρ τῶν ἁμαρτιῶν ἡμῶν __________ τὰς γραφάς.
7. God judges the hidden things of men according to my Gospel.
   κρίνει ὁ θεὸς τὰ κρυπτὰ τῶν ἀνθρώπων ________ τὸ εὐαγγέλιόν μου.
8. The workman dug around the fig-tree.
   ὁ ἐργάτης ἔσκαψεν ________ τὴν συκῆν.
9. Nathanael was under the fig-tree.
   Ναθαναὴλ ἦν _________ τὴν συκῆν.
10. The seed fell upon the ground.
    ὁ σπόρος ἔπεσεν ________ τῆς γῆς.
11. We have a house by the side of the road.
    οἶκον ἔχομεν _________ τὴν ὁδόν.

12. We received these commandments from the king.
ἐλάβομεν τὰς ἐντολὰς ταύτας ________ τοῦ βασιλέως.

13. I was in the temple every day.
__________ ἡμέραν ἤμην ἐν τῷ ἱερῷ.

14. The crowd marveled about his words.
ὁ ὄχλος ἐθαύμασεν _________ τῶν λόγων αὐτοῦ.

15. The brothers will pray to God for us.
οἱ ἀδελφοὶ προσεύξονται τῷ θεῷ _________ ἡμῶν.

16. Jesus will come on the clouds.
ἐλεύσεται ὁ Ἰησοῦς _________ τῶν νεφελῶν.

17. Paul sent the brother to us.
ὁ Παῦλος ἔπεμψεν τὸν ἀδελφὸν _________ ἡμᾶς.

18. The stones fell on them.
οἱ λίθοι ἔπεσον _______ αὐτούς.

19. The king sat on the throne.
ὁ βασιλεὺς ἐκάθητο ________ τῷ θρόνῳ.

20. Jesus dined with the tax-collectors.
ἠρίστα ὁ Ἰησοῦς __________ τοῖς τελώναις.

21. For the sake of this I bend my knees to the Father.
τούτου __________ κάμπτω τὰ γόνατά μου ________ τὸν πατέρα.

22. Jesus dined with the women.
ἠρίστα ὁ Ἰησοῦς __________ τῶν γυναικῶν.

23. I fell before his feet.
ἔπεσα ________ τῶν ποδῶν αὐτοῦ.

24. The scripture is being fulfilled in our ears.
πληροῦται ἡ γραφὴ _______ τοῖς ὠσὶν ἡμῶν.

Exercise 26-B: Put an X in the ( ) before the English expression which correctly renders the Greek:

1. μετὰ τοῦ ἀνδρός
( ) by the man
( ) to the man
( ) for the man
( ) with the man

2. κατὰ τῶν γραφῶν
( ) according to the scriptures
( ) against the scriptures
( ) on the scriptures
( ) in the scriptures

3. ὑπὲρ ἡμᾶς
( ) because of us
( ) by us
( ) over us
( ) under us

4. παρ' ἡμῶν
( ) with us
( ) after us
( ) from us
( ) for us

5. παρ' αὐτοῖς
( ) upon them
( ) with them
( ) over them
( ) under them

6. πρὸς ὑμᾶς
( ) on account of you
( ) on your behalf
( ) among you
( ) with you

7. δι' ἐμοῦ.
( ) to me
( ) for me
( ) by me
( ) according to me

8. μετὰ τοῦτο
( ) on this
( ) after this
( ) under this
( ) by this

9. διὰ τοῦτο
( ) through this
( ) because of this
( ) beside this
( ) without this

10. μετ' αὐτῆς

( ) with her
( ) after her
( ) against her
( ) according to her

11. καθ' ἡμέραν

( ) in a day
( ) every day
( ) for a day
( ) after a day

12. περὶ τῆς πόλεως

( ) around the city
( ) concerning the city
( ) near the city
( ) from the city

13. παρ' ἐμοί

( ) by my side
( ) for my sake
( ) in my stead
( ) in my interest

14. ὑπὸ τὴν ἐξουσίαν αὐτοῦ

( ) by his authority
( ) under his authority
( ) over his authority
( ) beyond his authority

Exercises to Lesson Twenty-Seven

Exercise 27-A: Study the paradigms of δίδωμι, τίθημι and ἵστημι, and complete the statements below. (Note: Some of the statements have been completed already; use these as guides.)

1. The stem-vowel in the present tense of μι-verbs is zero.
2. The present stem (= base) of δίδωμι is διδο (Cf. Pars. 164-169)
3. The present stem (= base) of τίθημι is ______
4. The present stem (= base) of ἵστημι is ______
5. The Primary A suffixes for μι-verbs (which occur only in the present active; the suffixes in the future are the same as those for λύω; see Pars. 169(1), 200(1)) are as follows:

Sg. 1.	μι	Pl. 1.	______
2.	______	2.	______
3.	______	3.	ασι (ν)

6. Before the singular Primary A suffixes,
   (a) the final ο of the stem διδο is changed to ______
   (b) the final ε of the stem τιθε is changed to ______
   (c) the final α of the stem ἱστα is changed to ______
7. Final α of ἱστα and initial α of suffix ασι(ν) are contracted to ____, so that the present active 3rd plural form of ἵστημι is ____________
8. The Primary B suffixes for μι-verbs (present only) are (cf. Pars. 169(2), 200(4)):

Sg. 1. ______ Pl. 1. ______

2. σαι 2. ______

3. ______ 3. ______

9. Is the final vowel of the present stem of any μι-verb altered before any of the Primary B suffixes? ________ (Yes or No)

10. Before the singular Secondary A suffixes,

(a) the final ο of the stem διδο is changed to ου

(b) the final ε of the stem τιθε is changed to ______ (1st person) or ______ (2nd and 3rd)

(c) the final α of the stem ἱστα is changed to ______

11. The forms of the Secondary A suffixes for the imperfect active of μι-verbs are exactly the same as they are for the ________ ________________ of ω-verbs. (Examine the relevant paradigms carefully, bearing in mind your answer to question 10, above.) The forms of the Secondary A suffixes for the imperfect active of μι-verbs are, therefore, as follows:

Sg. 1. ______ Pl. 1. ______

2. ______ 2. ______

3. ______ 3. ______

12. The forms of the Secondary A suffixes for the first aorist of μι-verbs are exactly the same as they are for the __________ ________________ of ω-verbs, namely:

Sg. 1. ______ Pl. 1. ______

2. ______ 2. ______

3. ______ 3. ______

13. The forms of the Secondary A suffixes for the second aorist of μι-verbs are those listed in question ______ above (11or 12)

14. There is no ν-movable in the 3rd sg. of the imperfect active of μι-verbs because ν-movable may follow only ______ or ______ (cf. Par. 169, Remark 1)

15. The (unaugmented) aorist middle stem of δίδωμι is δο

16. The (unaugmented) aorist middle stem of τίθημι is ______

17. The Secondary B suffixes for the aorist middle of μι-verbs are the same as they are for the aorist middle of ω-verbs, as follows:

Sg. 1.	______	Pl. 1.	______
2.	______	2.	______
3.	______	3.	______

The final vowel of the stem is dropped before the suffix ______

18. The Secondary B suffixes for the imperfect middle of μι-verbs are added to the augmented present stem (ἐδιδο-, ἐτιθε-, ἱστα-), and are as follows:

Sg. 1.	______	Pl. 1.	______
2.	______	2.	______
3.	______	3.	______

19. The Secondary B suffixes for the imperfect middle of μι-verbs and those for the aorist middle of μι-verbs are the same, except for the suffix of the ______ (1st, 2nd, 3rd) person ______ (Sg. or Pl.)

Exercise 27-B: Put an X in each appropriate space below; imitate the model:

	Person			Number		Pres.	Impf	Fut	Aor	Act	Mid. or Pass.	Mid. only	Pass. only
	1	2	3	Sg	Pl								
Model: ἔδοτο			X	X					X			X	
1. ἵστησι(ν)													
2. δίδομαι													
3. τίθημι													
4. δίδως													
5. ἐδίδου													
6. ἵσταται													
7. ἵστατο													
8. τιθέασιν													
9. ἔθηκεν													
10. δοθήσεται													
11. ἐτήθημεν													
12. τίθεται													
13. ἐδώκατε													
14. ἔθετο													
15. ἔστην													
16. ἔθου													
17. διδόμεθα													
18. τεθήσεται													
19. ἐδίδοτο													
20. ἔστησαν													

Exercise 27-C: Fill in the blank spaces in the table below, imitating the model given:

	Present Active	Imperfect Active	Aorist Active	Present Mid.&Pass.	Imperfect Mid.&Pass.	Aorist Middle
Model:	δίδωμι	ἐδίδουν	ἔδωκα	δίδομαι	ἐδιδόμην	ἐδόμην
1.	τίθης					
2.		ἐδίδομεν				
3.			ἔθηκα			
4.				δίδοται		
5.					ἐτιθέμεθα	
6.				τίθεται		
7.						ἔθεντο
8.	ἵσταμεν		1st 2nd			(None)
9.			ἔστησας ἔστης			(None)
10.		ἐτίθετε				
11.	ἵστησι(ν)		1st 2nd			(None)
12.					ἐδίδοσο	
13.			1st 2nd	ἵστασθε		(None)
14.			1st & 2nd ἔστησαν			(None)
15.	διδόασιν					

<u>Exercise 27-D</u>: Fill in the blank spaces in the table below, imitating the model given:

Future Active	Future Middle	Future Passive	Aorist Passive
Model: δώσω	δώσομαι	δοθήσομαι	ἐδόθην
1. θήσεις			
2.	θησόμεθα		
3.		σταθήσονται	
4.			ἐτέθη
5. στήσεις			
6.	στήσεται		
7.		τεθήσεσθε	
8.			ἐτέθησαν
9. δώσουσιν			
10.	δώσῃ		

<u>Exercise 27-E</u>: Write, in the blank space provided, the correct form of δίδωμι

(a) in the present tense, active voice:

1. ἐγώ σοι τὸν ἄρτον ____________

2. ὁ ἀνὴρ ταῦτά μοι ____________

3. ὑμεῖς τοῖς πτωχοῖς ἱμάτια ______________

4. ἡμεῖς ὑμῖν ἐκεῖνα __________________

5. νόμους ἡμῖν ________________ οἱ γραμματεῖς.

6. σὺ αὐτῷ μάχαιραν ___________

(b) in the imperfect active:

1. σὺ τὴν γνώμην σου ____________ μοι.

2. δόξαν τῷ θεῷ ἡμεῖς ________________

3. οἱ υἱοί μου ἰχθύν σοι ________________

4. τόπον τῇ ὀργῇ ______________ ὑμεῖς.

5. ἐγὼ τὴν τροφὴν τοῖς πένησιν _______________

6. ὁ ποιμὴν ἡμῖν ἀρνίον ________________

(c) in the aorist active:

1. τὸ ποτήριον ἡμῖν ____________ ὁ κύριος ἡμῶν.

2. ἐντολὰς καινὰς ὑμεῖς _______________ αὐτοῖς.

3. τῷ κλέπτῃ ἀργύριον ἐγὼ ____________

4. τοῖς τέκνοις αὐτῶν ἄρτους _____________ αἱ μητέρες.

5. αὐταῖς σὺ τοῦτο _______________

6. ἡμεῖς τοῖς ἀδελφοῖς οἶνον _________________

(d) in the future active:

1. σημεῖον τῷ λαῷ ἡμεῖς ______________

2. τὸν λόγον τοῦτον ________________ οἱ μαθηταὶ τοῖς ἱερεῦσιν.

3. σὺ πλοῖον αὐτῷ ________________

4. μισθόν σοι ἐγὼ _____________

5. ὁ ἁμαρτωλός μοι τὸ ἱμάτιον ______________

6. ὑμεῖς ἡμῖν εἰρήνην __________________

Exercise 27-F: Write, in the blank space provided, the correct form of τίθημι

(a) in the present active:

1. ἐγὼ τὸν λύχνον ἐπὶ τὴν λυχνίαν ____________
2. ὁ κύριος τὰς χεῖρας ἐπὶ τοὺς ὀφθαλμοὺς τοῦ τυφλοῦ ___________
3. οἱ μαθηταὶ αὐτοῦ αὐτὸν ἐν μνημείῳ ______________
4. σὺ αὐτὸ ὑπὸ τὸν μόδιον ______________
5. ἡμεῖς ὑπὲρ ὑμῶν τὰς ψυχὰς ἡμῶν _____________
6. ὑμεῖς αὐτὰ ἐν τῷ οἴκῳ ______________

(b) in the imperfect active:

1. ἐγὼ θεμέλιον ἐπὶ τὴν πέτραν ________________
2. Μωϋσῆς κάλυμμα ἐπὶ τὸ πρόσωπον _____________
3. σὺ τὴν δεξιάν σου ἐπ' ἐμὲ _________________
4. οἱ ἄνδρες τὸν στέφανον ἐπὶ τὴν κεφαλὴν αὐτοῦ _______________
5. ἡμεῖς τοὺς λύχνους ἐπὶ τὰς λυχνίας _______________
6. αὐτοὺς ὑπὸ τοὺς μοδίους ὑμεῖς _________________

(c) in the aorist active:

1. ὁ ποιμὴν τὴν ψυχὴν αὐτοῦ ὑπὲρ τῶν προβάτων _____________
2. ἡμεῖς ὑμᾶς ἀποστόλους ______________
3. ἐγώ σε κήρυκά μου ____________
4. σὺ κάλυμμα ἐπὶ τὸ πρόσωπόν σου _____________
5. ὑμεῖς τὸν στέφανον ἐπ' αὐτὸν _____________
6. οἱ μαθηταὶ αὐτοῦ αὐτὸν ἐν μνημείῳ _____________

(d) in the future active:

1. ὁ Χριστὸς τὸ πνεῦμα αὐτοῦ ἐφ' ἡμᾶς ____________

2. ἡμεῖς καινὸν θεμέλιον ______________

3. ἐγὼ ὑμᾶς βασιλεῖς καὶ ἱερεῖς ______________

4. ὑμεῖς τὰς ψυχὰς ὑμῶν ὑπὲρ αὐτῶν ______________

5. αὐτοὶ τὰς ψυχὰς αὐτῶν ὑπὲρ ὑμῶν ______________

6. ἐφ' ἡμᾶς αὐτὸ σὺ ______________

(e) in the aorist middle:

1. ἐγὼ τοὺς κλέπτας ἐν τῇ φυλακῇ ______________

2. οἱ στρατιῶται Παῦλον ἐν τῇ φυλακῇ ______________

3. σύ με ἐν τῇ φυλακῇ ______________

4. ὁ βασιλεὺς τὸν Ἰωάννην ἐν τῇ φυλακῇ ______________

5. ἡμεῖς ὑμᾶς ἐν τῇ φυλακῇ ______________

6. ὑμεῖς ἡμᾶς ἐν τῇ φυλακῇ ______________

<u>Exercise 27-G</u>: Write, in the blank space provided, the correct form of ἵστημι

(a) in the present active:

1. ὁ κύριος τοὺς μαθητὰς αὐτοῦ ἐν τῇ ἀληθείᾳ ______________

2. ἐγὼ αὐτὸν ἐπὶ τὴν γῆν ______________

3. σὺ αὐτὴν ἐπὶ τὴν γῆν ______________

4. ἡμεῖς ὑμᾶς ἐν τῇ ἐκκλησίᾳ ______________

5. αὐτοὺς ὑμεῖς ἐν τῇ ἐκκλησίᾳ ______________

6. οἱ γραμματεῖς τὰς παραδόσεις ______________

(b) in the imperfect active:

1. τὸ παιδίον ἐν μέσῳ τῶν μαθητῶν ______________ ὁ Ἰησοῦς.

2. σὺ ἡμᾶς ἐν τῇ ἀληθείᾳ ______________

3. ἐν τῷ λόγῳ μου ______________ ἐγὼ τοὺς μαθητάς μου.

4. αὐτοὺς ἡμεῖς ἐν τῷ λόγῳ ______________

5. ἐν τῷ εὐαγγελίῳ ______________ αὐτοὺς ὑμεῖς.

6. τὰς ἐκκλησίας ______________ οἱ ἀπόστολοι.

(c) in the <u>first</u> aorist active:

1. ὁ βασιλεὺς τὸ βδέλυγμα τῆς ἐρημώσεως ἐν τόπῳ ἁγίῳ ______________

2. σὺ εἴδωλον ἐν τῷ ἱερῷ ______________

3. εἴδωλα ἡμεῖς ______________ ἐν τῷ ναῷ.

4. αὐτὰ ἐπὶ τοὺς στύλους ______________ ὑμεῖς.

5. ἐπὶ πέτραν σε ______________ ἐγώ.

6. λίθον πρὸ τοῦ μνημείου οἱ στρατιῶται ______________

(d) in the future:

1. ἐγὼ αὐτοὺς διὰ τοῦ λόγου μου ______________
2. ἡμᾶς ἐν τῇ ἀληθείᾳ σὺ ______________
3. βδελύγματα ἐν τῷ ἱερῷ ______________ ὑμεῖς.
4. αὐτὰ παρὰ τὴν ὁδὸν ______________ ἡμεῖς.
5. τὸν θρόνον αὐτοῦ ______________ ὁ βασιλεὺς πρὸ τοῦ ναοῦ.
6. οἱ ἐχθροὶ αὐτοῦ ἐν μέσῳ τῶν βασανιστῶν ______________ αὐτόν.

(e) in the second aorist:

1. ἐπὶ τὸ ὄρος Σιὼν ______________ τὸ ἀρνίον.
2. ἐγὼ ἐπὶ τοῦ τόπου ἐκείνου______________
3. οἱ μαθηταὶ ἐνώπιον τοῦ κυρίου ______________
4. ἐπὶ τοὺς πόδας ἡμῶν ______________ ἡμεῖς.
5. ὑμεῖς πρὸ τῶν θυρῶν ______________
6. σὺ πρὸ τοῦ βασιλέως ______________

(f) in the aorist passive:

1. ἐγὼ πρὸ τοῦ ἡγεμόνος ______________
2. ἐπὶ τῶν τόπων ὑμῶν τῶν ὑψηλῶν ______________ ἡμεῖς.
3. ἔμπροσθεν τοῦ βασιλέως ______________ ὑμεῖς.
4. ἐν τῇ ἡμέρᾳ ἐκείνῃ ______________ σὺ ἐπὶ τῆς γῆς.
5. τὸ παιδίον εἰς τὸ μέσον ______________
6. αἱ ἀδελφαὶ ἀνὰ μέσον τῶν μαθητῶν ______________

(g) in the future passive:

1. ἐγὼ διὰ τῆς δυνάμεώς σου ______________
2. ἡμεῖς ἐπὶ τῶν ὀρέων ______________
3. ἐνώπιον τῶν ἀρχόντων ______________ ὑμεῖς.
4. μεθ' ἡμῶν σὺ ______________
5. παρὰ τοῖς μαθηταῖς ______________ ὁ διδάσκαλος.
6. οἱ μαθηταὶ πρὸ τοῦ διδασκάλου ______________

Exercise 27-H: Making use of the Vocabulary below, translate the following sentences into English:

ἀλήθεια, ας, ἡ, truth	μισθός, οῦ, ὁ, reward
βασιλεύς. έως, ὁ, king	παιδίον, ου, τὸ, child
θεός, οῦ, ὁ, God	πατήρ, πατρός, ὁ, father
κεφαλή, ῆς, ἡ, head	σημεῖον, ου, τὸ, sign
κύριος, ου, ὁ, Lord	στέφανος, ου, ὁ, crown
λόγος, ου, ὁ, word	υἱός, οῦ, ὁ, son
μαθητής, οῦ, ὁ, disciple	φυλακή, ῆς, ἡ, prison
μέσον, ου, τὸ, middle, midst	ψυχή, ῆς, ἡ, soul, life
(ἐν μέσῳ + gen. = in the midst of)	(τίθημι τὴν ψυχήν μου = I lay down my life)

1. ὁ κύριος τοῖς μαθηταῖς αὐτοῦ ἔδωκεν σημεῖον.

____

2. τὸ σημεῖον τοῦτο ἐδόθη αὐτοῖς.

____

3. παιδίον ἔστησεν ἐν μέσῳ αὐτῶν.

____

4. τὸ παιδίον ἔστη ἐν μέσῳ αὐτῶν.

____

5. τὴν ψυχὴν αὐτοῦ ἔθηκεν ὑπὲρ αὐτῶν.

____

6. ἔθεντο τοῦτον τὸν μαθητὴν ἐν τῇ φυλακῇ.

____

7. μισθὸς δοθήσεται αὐτοῖς.

____

8. τὸν μισθὸν δώσει αὐτοῖς ὁ βασιλεύς.

____

9. τὸν στέφανον αὐτοῦ θήσει ἐπὶ τὴν κεφαλὴν αὐτοῦ.

____

10. οἱ μαθηταὶ τεθήσονται υἱοὶ θεοῦ.

____

11. βασιλέα τίθησιν τὸν υἱὸν αὐτοῦ.

12. τεθήσομαι μαθητής σου διὰ τοῦ λόγου σου.

13. ἡμᾶς στήσει ἐνώπιον τοῦ πατρὸς αὐτοῦ.

14. διὰ τοῦ λόγου αὐτοῦ σταθησόμεθα.

15. τὰς ψυχὰς ἡμῶν θήσομεν διὰ τοὺς λόγους αὐτοῦ.

16. σημεῖα ἐδίδοντο τῷ βασιλεῖ.

17. σημεῖα ἐδίδοσαν τῷ βασιλεῖ.

18. ὁ στέφανος τοῦ βασιλέως τῷ παιδίῳ δίδοται.

19. ὁ βασιλεὺς τῷ παιδίῳ δίδωσι τὸ στέφανον αὐτοῦ.

20. ἐστάθη πρὸ τοῦ βασιλέως τὸ παιδίον.

21. ἐδίδου ὁ κύριος αὐτοῖς τοὺς λόγους τῆς ἀληθείας.

22. ὁ στέφανος ἐτέθη ἐπὶ τὴν κεφαλὴν τοῦ βασιλέως.

23. ὁ υἱὸς τοῦ βασιλέως τίθεται μαθητὴς κυρίου.

24. στέφανοι δοθήσονται ὑμῖν ὑπὸ τοῦ πατρὸς ὑμῶν.

25. μαθητὰς ἔθου τὰ παιδία.

Exercises to Lesson Twenty-Eight

Exercise 28-A: Give the present active participle of the following verbs, in the gender, number and case required (imitate the model):

Model: πιστεύω	masc.	sg.	nom.	πιστεύων
1. λέγω	"	"	"	______
2. ἔχω	"	"	gen.	______
3. ποιέω (ποιῶ)	"	"	dat.	______
4. ἀκούω	"	"	acc.	______
5. γινώσκω	"	pl.	nom.	______
6. δίδωμι	"	"	gen.	______
7. λαλέω (λαλῶ)	"	"	dat.	______
8. γράφω	"	"	acc.	______
9. ἐσθίω	fem.	sg.	nom.	______
10. εὑρίσκω	"	"	gen.	______
11. ἵστημι	"	"	dat.	______
12. ἀγαπάω (ἀγαπῶ)	"	"	acc.	______
13. βλέπω	"	pl.	nom.	______
14. ζάω (ζῶ)	"	"	gen.	______
15. καλέω (καλῶ)	"	"	dat.	______
16. ζητέω (ζητῶ)	"	"	acc.	______
17. σώζω	neut.	sg.	nom.	______
18. ὁράω (ὁρῶ)	"	"	gen.	______
19. εἰμί	"	"	dat.	______
20. γεννάω (γεννῶ)	"	"	acc.	______
21. διδάσκω	"	pl.	nom.	______

22. αἴρω	neut. pl. gen.		____________
23. μένω	" " dat.		____________
24. τίθημι	" " acc.		____________

Exercise 28-B: Give the present middle or passive participle for each of the following verbs, in the gender, number and case required (imitate the model):

Model: λύω	masc. sg. nom.	λυόμενος
1. τίθημι	" " gen.	____________
2. ἀγαπάω (ἀγαπῶ)	" pl. dat.	____________
3. ποιέω (ποιῶ)	" " acc.	____________
4. ἵστημι	fem. sg. nom.	____________
5. λέγω	" " gen.	____________
6. γράφω	" pl. nom.	____________
7. δίδωμι	" " dat.	____________
8. πληρόω (πληρῶ)	" " acc.	____________
9. βαπτίζω	neut. sg. nom.	____________
10. αἰτέω (αἰτῶ)	" pl. acc.	____________

Exercise 28-C: Give the present participle for each of the following deponent verbs, in the gender, number, and case required:

1. γίνομαι	masc. sg. nom.	____________
2. ἔρχομαι	" " dat.	____________
3. πορεύομαι	fem. pl. gen.	____________
4. προσεύχομαι	neut. sg. acc.	____________
5. ἀσπάζομαι	" pl. nom.	____________

Exercise 28-D: Transform the given sentences into sentences with equivalent meaning but with periphrastic constructions replacing the simple verbs (imitate the models).

Model (a): ὁ ἀνὴρ βαπτίζει τὸν παῖδα.
Transform: ὁ ἀνήρ ἐστιν βαπτίζων τὸν παῖδα.
Model (b): οἱ παῖδες ἐβαπτίζοντο ὑπὸ τοῦ ἀνδρός.
Transform: οἱ παῖδες ἦσαν βαπτιζόμενοι ὑπὸ τοῦ ἀνδρός.

1. ἐγὼ ἔγραφον ἐπιστολάς.

____

2. σὺ ζητήσεις τὴν βασιλείαν. (ζητέω)

____

3. ὁ πατὴρ σώζει ἡμᾶς.

____

4. ἡμεῖς ἠγαπώμεθα ὑπὸ τῶν ἀδελφῶν. (ἀγαπάω)

____

5. ὑμεῖς διδάξετε τοὺς μαθητάς. (διδασκω)

____

6. ἡ ἀδελφὴ ἔγραφεν ἐπιστολήν.

____

7. αἱ ἐπιστολαὶ γράφονται ὑπὸ τῶν ἀνδρων.

____

8. οἱ ἄνδρες γράφουσιν τὰς ἐπιστολάς.

____

<u>Exercise 28-E</u>: Complete the Greek sentences below so that they will correctly render the English sentences above them. Be guided by the models provided:

<u>Model</u> (a): He who believes (= he that believes, the one who believes) in the Son has eternal life.
ὁ πιστεύων εἰς τὸν υἱὸν ἔχει ζωὴν αἰώνιον.

<u>Model</u> (b): They that (= those who, the ones who) believe in the Son have eternal life.
οἱ πιστεύοντες εἰς τὸν υἱὸν ἔχουσι ζωὴν αἰώνιον.

<u>Model</u> (c): The widows who believe in the Son have eternal life.
αἱ χῆραι αἱ πιστεύουσαι εἰς τὸν υἱὸν ἔχουσι ζωὴν αἰώνιον.

1. We are seeking the disciples who believe in the Son.
ζητοῦμεν τοὺς μαθητὰς ____________________

2. They are seeking my daughter who believes in the Son.
ζητοῦσιν τὴν θυγατέρα μου ____________________

3. He is giving a new commandment to those who believe in the Son.
δίδωσιν καινὴν ἐντολὴν ____________________

4. We are receiving a new commandment from those who believe in the Son.
λαμβάνομεν καινὴν ἐντολὴν παρὰ ____________________

5. The words of those who believe in the Son are true.
ἀληθινοὶ οἱ λόγοι ____________________

6. He is coming with his sisters who believe in the Son.
ἔρχεται σὺν ταῖς ἀδελφαῖς αὐτοῦ ____________________

7. The child who believes in the Son has eternal life.
τὸ τέκνον ____________________ ἔχει ζωὴν αἰώνιον.

8. He is coming with his sisters who believe in the Son.
ἔρχεται μετὰ τῶν ἀδελφῶν αὐτοῦ ____________________

Exercise 28-F: Complete the Greek sentences below so that they will correctly render the English sentences above them. Be guided by the models provided; refer also to the models provided for Exercise 28-E:

Model (a): He who loves his brother fulfills the law.
ὁ ἀγαπῶν τὸν ἀδελφὸν αὐτοῦ πληροῖ τὸν νόμον.

Model (b): Those who love God hear the words of his Son.
οἱ ἀγαπῶντες τὸν θεὸν ἀκούουσι τοὺς λόγους τοῦ υἱοῦ αὐτοῦ.

Model (c): The child who loves God hears his Son.
τὸ τέκνον τὸ ἀγαπῶν τὸν θεὸν ἀκούει τὸν υἱὸν αὐτοῦ.

1. The law is being fulfilled by him who loves his brother.
ὁ νόμος πληροῦται ὑπὸ ______________________________

2. The children who love God hear his Son.
τὰ τέκνα ______________________ ἀκούουσι τὸν υἱὸν αὐτοῦ.

3. We are receiving these things from those who love God.
λαμβάνομεν ταῦτα παρὰ ______________________

4. We are giving those things to the widows who love God.
ἐκεῖνα δίδομεν ταῖς χήραις ______________________

5. God loves the man who loves his brother.
ὁ θεὸς ἀγαπᾷ τὸν ἄνδρα ______________________

6. The disciples love those who love God.
οἱ μαθηταὶ ἀγαπῶσιν ______________________

7. The disciples are coming with the children who love God.
οἱ μαθηταὶ ἔρχονται σὺν ______________________

8. He gives the cup to the disciple who loves his brother.
τὸ ποτήριον δίδωσι τῷ μαθητῇ ______________________

Exercise 28-G: Complete the Greek sentences below so that they will correctly render the English sentences above them. Be guided by the models provided; refer also to the models provided for the previous two exercises:

Model (a): He who does the will of my Father is my brother.

ὁ ποιῶν τὸ θέλημα τοῦ πατρός μού ἐστιν ἀδελφός μου.

Model (b): We who do the will of God are disciples of his Son.

ἡμεῖς οἱ ποιοῦντες τὸ θέλημα τοῦ θεοῦ ἐσμεν μαθηταὶ τοῦ υἱοῦ αὐτοῦ.

Model (c): The child who does the will of God is a child of God.

τὸ τέκνον τὸ ποιοῦν τὸ θέλημα τοῦ θεοῦ τέκνον θεοῦ ἐστιν.

1. I love those who do the will of my Father.

   ἀγαπῶ ____

2. I give peace to those who do the will of God.

   εἰρήνην δίδωμι ____

3. She who does the will of my Father is my sister.

   ____ ἐστιν ἀδελφή μου.

4. He is teaching for the sake of us who do the will of God.

   διδάσκει ὑπὲρ ἡμῶν ____

5. We are doing evil in the presence of him who does the will of God.

   κακὸν ποιοῦμεν ἔμπροσθεν ____

6. He is sending an apostle to the disciple who does the will of God.

   ἀπόστολον πέμπει τῷ μαθητῇ ____

7. The church which does the will of God is faithful.

   πιστὴ ἡ ἐκκλησία ____

8. We send an apostle to the church which does the will of God.

   πέμπομεν ἀπόστολον τῇ ἐκκλησίᾳ ____

Exercise 28-H: Complete the Greek sentences below so that they will correctly render the English sentences above them. Be guided by the models provided; refer also to the models provided for the previous three exercises:

Model (a): He who fulfills his ministry is a disciple.
ὁ πληρῶν τὴν διακονίαν αὐτοῦ μαθητής ἐστιν.

Model (b): He hears the word which fulfills the law of God.
ἀκούει τὸν λόγον τὸν πληροῦντα τὸν νόμον τοῦ θεοῦ.

Model (c): Those who fulfill their ministry are disciples.
οἱ πληροῦντες τὴν διακονίαν αὐτῶν μαθηταί εἰσιν.

1. Jesus loves disciples who fulfill their ministry.
ὁ Ἰησοῦς ἀγαπᾷ μαθητὰς τοὺς ______

2. The Lord speaks the word which fulfills the law.
λαλεῖ ὁ κύριος τὸν λόγον ______

3. This is the book of the words which fulfill the law.
τοῦτό ἐστιν τὸ βιβλίον τῶν λόγων ______

4. This is the new commandment which fulfills the law.
αὕτη ἐστὶν ἡ καινὴ ἐντολὴ ______

5. The Lord is preaching to the men who are fulfilling their ministry.
κηρύσσει ὁ κύριος τοῖς ἀνδράσιν ______

6. He preaches to the church which fulfills its ministry.
κηρύσσει τῇ ἐκκλησίᾳ ______

7. He gives us new commandments which fulfill the law.
δίδωσιν ἡμῖν ἐντολὰς καινὰς τὰς ______

8. This is the gospel which fulfills the law.
τοῦτό ἐστιν τὸ εὐαγγέλιον ______

<u>Exercise 28-I</u>: Complete the Greek sentences below so that they will correctly render the English sentences above them. Be guided by the models provided; refer also to the models provided for the previous four exercises:

<u>Model</u> (a): He who gives us this commandment is the Lord.
ὁ διδοὺς ἡμῖν ταύτην τὴν ἐντολήν ἐστιν ὁ κύριος.

<u>Model</u> (b): The church which gives us commandments is ancient.
ἀρχαία ἡ ἐκκλησία ἡ διδοῦσα ἡμῖν ἐντολάς.

<u>Model</u> (c): Those who give us commandments are apostles.
οἱ διδόντες ἡμῖν ἐντολάς εἰσιν ἀπόστολοι.

1. We love the Lord who gives us this commandment.
   ἀγαπῶμεν τὸν κύριον ______________________________

2. We are being loved by the Lord who gives us this commandment.
   ἀγαπώμεθα ὑπὸ τοῦ κυρίου ______________________________

3. We give glory to the Lord who gives us this commandment.
   δόξαν δίδομεν τῷ κυρίῳ ______________________________

4. We give glory to the church which gives us commandments.
   δόξαν δίδομεν τῇ ἐκκλησίᾳ ______________________________

5. We give glory to those who give us commandments.
   δόξαν δίδομεν τοῖς ______________________________

6. He is a disciple of the apostle who gives us commandments.
   μαθητής ἐστιν τοῦ ἀποστόλου ______________________________

7. He is coming from the church which gives us commandments.
   ἔρχεται ἀπὸ τῆς ἐκκλησίας ______________________________

8. He is a minister of the churches which give us commandments.
   διάκονός ἐστιν τῶν ἐκκλησιῶν ______________________________

Exercise 28-J: Complete the Greek sentences below so that they will correctly render the English sentences above them. Be guided by the models provided; refer also to the models provided for the previous five exercises:

Model (a): He who lays down his life for us is the Christ.
ὁ τιθεὶς τὴν ψυχὴν αὐτοῦ ὑπὲρ ἡμῶν ἐστιν ὁ Χριστός.

Model (b): The apostle who is laying a foundation is Paul.
ὁ ἀπόστολος ὁ τιθεὶς θεμέλιον Παῦλός ἐστιν.

Model (c): The sister who lays down her life is faithful.
ἡ ἀδελφὴ ἡ τιθεῖσα τὴν ψυχὴν αὐτῆς πιστή ἐστιν.

1. They are honoring the apostle who is laying a foundation.
τιμῶσι τὸν ἀπόστολον ______________________________

2. We give glory to Christ who lays down his life for us.
δόξαν δίδομεν τῷ Χριστῷ ______________________________

3. We give glory to the apostles who are laying a foundation.
δόξαν δίδομεν τοῖς ἀποστόλοις ______________________________

4. We give honor to the sister who lays down her life.
τιμὴν δίδομεν τῇ ἀδελφῇ ______________________________

5. We are beholding the glory of the Christ who lays down his life for us.
θεώμεθα τὴν δόξαν τοῦ Χριστοῦ ______________________________

6. You honor the apostles who are laying a foundation.
τιμᾶτε τοὺς ἀποστόλους ______________________________

7. We honor the father of the sisters who are laying a foundation.
τιμῶμεν τὸν πατέρα τῶν ἀδελφῶν ______________________________

8. He honors the child who is laying a foundation.
τιμᾷ τὸ τέκνον ______________________________

Exercise 28-K: Complete the Greek sentences below so that they will correctly translate the English sentences above them. Be guided by the models provided; refer also to the models provided for the previous six exercises:

Model (a): They that place us before the king are soldiers.

οἱ ἱστάντες ἡμᾶς ἔμπροσθεν τοῦ βασιλέως εἰσὶν στρατιῶται.

Model (b): He that places the child in the midst of the disciples is the Lord.

ὁ ἱστὰς τὸ παιδίον ἐν μέσῳ τῶν μαθητῶν ἐστιν ὁ κύριος.

Model (c): He who establishes his covenant with us is the Lord.

ὁ ἱστὰς τὴν διαθήκην αὐτοῦ πρὸς ἡμᾶς ἐστιν ὁ κύριος.

1. The disciples marvel at the Lord who places the child in their midst.

   οἱ μαθηταὶ θαυμάζουσι τὸν κύριον ____________________ ἐν μέσῳ αὐτῶν.

2. We give glory to God who establishes his covenant with us.

   δόξαν δίδομεν τῷ θεῷ ____________________________________

3. We fear the soldiers who place us before the king.

   φοβούμεθα τοὺς στρατιώτας ________________________________

4. We are disciples of the Lord who establishes his covenant with us.

   μαθηταί ἐσμεν τοῦ κυρίου __________________________________

5. He is sending a messenger to the soldiers who are placing us before the king.

   ἄγγελον πέμπει τοῖς στρατιώταις ____________________________

   ____

6. The disciples marvel at the mother who is placing her child in their midst.

   οἱ μαθηταὶ θαυμάζουσιν τὴν μητέρα ____________________________

   ____

Exercise 28-L: Complete the Greek sentences below so that they will correctly render the English sentences above them. Be guided by the models provided; refer also to the models provided for the previous seven exercises:

Model (a): He who is from God teaches us these things.
ὁ ὢν παρὰ τοῦ θεοῦ διδάσκει ἡμᾶς ταῦτα.

Model (b): The church which is in Corinth is faithful.
πιστὴ ἡ ἐκκλησία ἡ οὖσα ἐν Κορίνθῳ.

1. Those who are from Christ teach us these things.
οἱ _________ παρὰ τοῦ Χριστοῦ διδάσκουσιν ἡμᾶς ταῦτα.

2. We teach these things to the church which is in Corinth.
ταῦτα διδάσκομεν τὴν ἐκκλησίαν _________________________

3. They come from the churches which are in Asia.
ἔρχονται ἐκ τῶν ἐκκλησιῶν _________________ ἐν Ἀσίᾳ.

4. We send messengers to the churches which are in Asia.
ἀγγέλους πέμπομεν ταῖς ἐκκλησίαις _________________________

5. The child who is with Christ is blessed.
τὸ παιδίον μακάριον ___________ σὺν Χριστῷ.

6. We give these things to the men who are with Christ.
ταῦτα δίδομεν τοῖς ἀνδράσιν _________________________

7. Paul is writing to the church which is in Corinth.
Παῦλος γράφει τῇ ἐκκλησίᾳ _________________________

8. These are the words of the disciples who are with Christ.
οὗτοί εἰσιν οἱ λόγοι τῶν μαθητῶν _________________________

<u>Exercise 28-M</u>: Complete the Greek sentences below so that they will correctly render the English sentences above them. Be guided by the models provided; refer also to the models provided for the previous eight exercises:

<u>Model</u> (a): Blessed are those who are being saved.
μακάριοι οἱ σῳζόμενοι (σῴζω, save)

<u>Model</u> (b): These who are being led astray are blind.
τυφλοὶ οἱ πλανώμενοι. (πλανάω, lead astray)

<u>Model</u> (c): Blessed are those who are being called.
μακάριοι οἱ καλούμενοι. (καλέω, call)

<u>Model</u> (d): He who is being crucified is a robber.
λῃστής ἐστιν ὁ σταυρούμενος. (σταυρόω, crucify)

1. We give glory to those who are being saved.
   δόξαν δίδομεν ______________________________

2. We are seeking those who are being led astray.
   ζητοῦμεν ______________________________

3. Paul writes to the ministers who are being called.
   γράφει Παῦλος τοῖς διακόνοις ______________________________

4. They are dividing the clothes of the robber who is being crucified.
   διαμερίζονται τὰ ἱμάτια τοῦ λῃστοῦ ______________________________

5. He gives laws to those who are being led astray.
   νόμους δίδωσι ______________________________

6. Blessed is she who is being saved.
   μακαρία ______________________________

7. They give glory to the one who is being crucified for their sakes.
   δόξαν διδόασι ________________________ ὑπὲρ αὐτῶν.

8. The shepherd is seeking the sheep which is being led astray.
   ζητεῖ ὁ ποιμὴν τὸ πρόβατον ____________________________

Exercise 28-N: Complete the Greek sentences below so that they will correctly render the English sentences above them. Be guided by the models provided; refer also to the models provided for the previous nine exercises:

Model (a): This is the prophet who is coming into the world.
οὗτός ἐστιν ὁ προφήτης ὁ ἐρχόμενος εἰς τὸν κόσμον.

Model (b): The commandment which is being given to us is new.
ἡ ἐντολὴ ἡ διδομένη ἡμῖν καινή ἐστιν.

1. We are disciples of the prophet who is coming into the world.
   μαθηταί ἐσμεν τοῦ προφήτου ______________________________

2. We are keeping the commandment which is being given to us.
   τηροῦμεν τὴν ἐντολὴν ________________________________

3. You keep the commandments which are being given to you.
   τηρεῖσθε τὰς ἐντολὰς ________________________ ὑμῖν.

4. The law which is being given to the people is new.
   καινὸς ὁ νόμος ____________________ τῷ λαῷ.

5. He is teaching the children who are coming into the city.
   διδάσκει τὰ τέκνα ____________________ εἰς τὴν πόλιν.

6. He who comes in that day is greater than John.
   μείζων Ἰωάννου ἐστὶν __________________ ἐν ἐκείνῃ τῇ ἡμέρᾳ.

7. We have eternal life which comes from the Father.

   ἔχομεν ζωὴν αἰώνιον ______________________ παρὰ τοῦ πατρός.

8. We have the law which is being given to you.

   ἔχομεν τὸν νόμον ____

Exercises to Lesson Twenty-Nine

Exercise 29-A: Complete the Greek sentences below so that they will correctly render the English sentences above them. Be guided by the models provided:

Model (a): While he is saying these things the apostle baptizes the disciples.

λέγων ταῦτα βαπτίζει τοὺς μαθητὰς ὁ ἀπόστολος.

Model (b): While he was saying these things the apostle baptized the disciples.

λέγων ταῦτα ἐβάπτιζεν τοὺς μαθητὰς ὁ ἀπόστολος.

1. The disciples are being baptized by the apostle while he says these things.

   βαπτίζονται οἱ μαθηταὶ ὑπὸ τοῦ ἀποστόλου ταῦτα ______________

2. The disciples were being baptized by the apostle while he was saying these things.

   ἐβαπτίζοντο οἱ μαθηταὶ ὑπὸ τοῦ ἀποστόλου ταῦτα ______________

3. The disciples gave praise to the apostle while he was saying these things.

   αἶνον ἐδίδοσαν οἱ μαθηταὶ τῷ ἀποστόλῳ ταῦτα ______________

4. The disciples honored the apostle as he was saying these things.

   ἐτίμων οἱ μαθηταὶ τὸν ἀπόστολον ταῦτα ______________

5. The brother honored the sister as she was saying these things.

   ἐτίμα ὁ ἀδελφὸς τὴν ἀδελφὴν ταῦτα ______________

6. The disciples marveled at the child as he was saying these things.

   ἐθαύμαζον οἱ μαθηταὶ τὸ παιδίον ταῦτα ______________

7. The disciple honored the apostles as they were saying these things.

   ἐτίμα ὁ μαθητὴς τοὺς ἀποστόλους ταῦτα ______________

8. The disciple gives praise to the apostles while they are saying these things.

   αἶνον δίδωσιν ὁ μαθητὴς τοῖς ἀποστόλοις ταῦτα ________________

<u>Exercise 29-B</u>: Complete the Greek sentences below so that they will correctly render the English sentences above them. Be guided by the models provided:

<u>Model</u> (a): While they are hungering for righteousness the Lord teaches them.

πεινῶντας τὴν δικαιοσύνην διδάσκει αὐτοὺς ὁ κύριος.

<u>Model</u> (b): While they were seeking the Lord, he found them.

εὗρεν αὐτοὺς ζητοῦντας τὸν κύριον.

<u>Model</u> (c): When they fulfill his commandments, he will be with them.

ἔσται σὺν αὐτοῖς πληροῦσιν τὰς ἐντολὰς αὐτοῦ.

1. The Lord gave bread to them while they were hungry (=hungering).

   ἐδίδου αὐτοῖς ἄρτον ὁ κύριος ____________________

2. He pursues them while they are seeking the Lord.

   αὐτοὺς διώκει ____________________ τὸν κύριον.

3. He will give them the kingdom when they fulfill his commandments.

   τὴν βασιλείαν δώσει αὐτοῖς ________________ τὰς ἐντολὰς αὐτοῦ.

4. He will be with them when they are seeking the Lord.

   ἔσται μετ' αὐτῶν ________________ τὸν κύριον.

5. We shall teach them because they are hungering for righteousness.

   αὐτοὺς διδάξομεν ____________________ τὴν δικαιοσύνην.

6. When they fulfill his commandments they will be with him.

   ἔσονται σὺν αὐτῷ ____________________ τὰς ἐντολὰς αὐτοῦ.

7. While they were seeking the Lord they were taught by him.
   ____________________ τὸν κύριον ἐδιδάσκοντο ὑπ᾽αὐτοῦ.

8. He taught me when I was hungering for righteousness.
   ἐδίδασκέ με ____________________ τὴν δικαιοσύνην.

Exercise 29-C: Complete the Greek sentences below so that they will correctly render the English sentences above them. Be guided by the models provided:

Model (a): He healed us while he was giving good things to the poor.
ἐθεράπευσεν ἡμᾶς διδοὺς καλὰ τοῖς πτωχοῖς.

Model (b): When he puts his spirit upon us he makes us disciples.
μαθητὰς ἡμᾶς ποιεῖ τιθεὶς τὸ πνεῦμα αὐτοῦ ἐφ᾽ἡμᾶς.

Model (c): He saves us as he establishes his covenant with us.
ἡμᾶς σῴζει ἱστὰς τὴν διαθήκην αὐτοῦ πρὸς ἡμᾶς.

1. They glorify him as he gives good things to the poor.
   δοξάζουσιν αὐτὸν ____________________ καλὰ τοῖς πτωχοῖς.

2. We were with him when he was giving good things to the poor.
   ἤμεθα σὺν αὐτῷ ____________________ καλὰ τοῖς πτωχοῖς.

3. We are his disciples because he puts his spirit upon us.
   μαθηταὶ αὐτοῦ ἐσμεν ____________________ τὸ πνεῦμα αὐτοῦ ἐφ᾽ἡμᾶς.

4. We glorify God as he establishes his covenant with us.
   δοξάζομεν τὸν θεὸν ____________________________________

5. He healed them while they were giving good things to the poor.
   ἐθεράπευεν αὐτοὺς ____________________________________

6. We give him glory because he puts his spirit upon us.
   δόξαν δίδομεν αὐτῷ ____________________________________

7. We give glory to God while he establishes his covenant with us.
   δόξαν τῷ θεῷ δίδομεν ________________________________

8. We shall be with them while they are establishing a covenant with us.
   ἐσόμεθα μετ' αὐτῶν ________________________________

Exercise 29-D: Complete the Greek sentences below so that they will correctly render the English sentences above them. Be guided by the models provided:

Model (a): While we are in the world we are being saved by Christ.
σῳζόμεθα ὑπὸ τοῦ Χριστοῦ ἐν τῷ κόσμῳ ὄντες.

Model (b): As he comes into the world he will save us.
εἰς τὸν κόσμον ἐρχόμενος σώσει ἡμᾶς.

1. Christ saves us while we are in the world.
ὁ Χριστὸς σῴζει ἡμᾶς ______________________________

2. We shall be saved by Christ as he comes into the world.
σωθησόμεθα ὑπὸ τοῦ Χριστοῦ ______________________________

3. While he was in the world he saved sinners.
______________________________ ἔσῳζεν ἁμαρτωλούς.

4. We give glory to him as he comes into the world.
δόξαν δίδομεν αὐτῷ ______________________________

5. We give glory to him while he is in the world.
δόξαν δίδομεν αὐτῷ ______________________________

6. He is our saviour while we are in the world.
ἔστιν σωτὴρ ἡμῶν ______________________________

7. We are in the church while it is in the world.
ἐν τῇ ἐκκλησίᾳ ἐσμὲν ______________________________

8. He saved the church when he was in the world.
τὴν ἐκκλησίαν ἔσῳζεν ______________________________

9. He saves the church while it is in the world.
τὴν ἐκκλησίαν σῴζει ______________________________

10. He saves the children as they come into the world.

    τὰ τέκνα σῴζει ______________________________

Exercise 29-E: Complete the Greek sentences below so that they will correctly render the English sentences above them. Be guided by the models provided:

Model (a): While they were being baptized by the apostle the disciples glorified God.

βαπτιζόμενοι ὑπὸ τοῦ ἀποστόλου οἱ μαθηταὶ ἐδόξαζον τὸν θεόν.

Model (b): The shepherd seeks the sheep while they are being led astray by the wicked hireling.

ὁ ποιμὴν ζητεῖ τὰ πρόβατα ὑπὸ τοῦ πονηροῦ μισθωτοῦ πλανώμενα.

Model (c): They glorified Jesus because he was being crucified for them.

ἐδόξαζον τὸν Ἰησοῦν ὑπὲρ αὐτῶν σταυρούμενον.

1. The hireling leads the sheep astray while they are being sought by the shepherd.

   ὁ μισθωτὸς πλανᾷ τὰ πρόβατα ὑπὸ τοῦ ποιμένος ______________

2. While he was being crucified for us Jesus glorified God.

   ἐδόξαζεν τὸν θεὸν ὁ Ἰησοῦς ὑπὲρ ἡμῶν ______________

3. We taught the disciples while they were being baptized by you.

   ἐδιδάσκομεν τοὺς μαθητὰς ὑφ' ὑμῶν ______________

4. We gave this to the shepherds while they were being sought by the faithful hireling.

   τοῦτο ἐδίδομεν τοῖς ποιμέσιν ὑπὸ τοῦ πιστοῦ μισθωτοῦ ______________

5. He gave white garments to the sisters while they were being baptized by the apostle.

   λευκὰ ἱμάτια ἐδίδου ταῖς ἀδελφαῖς ὑπὸ τοῦ ἀποστόλου ______________

6. I am seeking the shepherd of the sheep because they are being led astray by the wicked hireling.

ζητῶ τὸν ποιμένα τῶν προβάτων ὑπὸ τοῦ πονηροῦ μισθωτοῦ ____________

7. They are dividing his garments while he is being crucified for us.

διαμερίζονται τὰ ἱμάτια αὐτοῦ ὑπὲρ ἡμῶν ____________________

8. He gave wine to Jesus while he was being crucified for us.

οἶνον τῷ 'Ιησοῦ ἐδίδου ____________________ ὑπὲρ ἡμῶν.

<u>Exercise 29-F</u>: Complete the Greek sentences below so that they will correctly render the English sentences above them. Be guided by the models provided:

<u>Model</u> (a): While we were in the city the chief priest was leading the people astray.
ἡμῶν ἐν τῇ πόλει ὄντων ἐπλάνα τὸν λαὸν ὁ ἀρχιερεύς.

<u>Model</u> (b): When we come into the city you will know the truth.
ἡμῶν ἐρχομένων εἰς τὴν πόλιν γνώσεσθε τὴν ἀλήθειαν.

<u>Model</u> (c): While Peter was speaking these things the Lord stood in the midst of the disciples. (ἔστη, from ἵστημι)

ταῦτα λαλοῦντος τοῦ Πέτρου ἔστη ὁ κύριος ἐν μέσῳ τῶν μαθητῶν.

1. We were in the city while the chief priest was leading the people astray.

ἐν τῇ πόλει ἦμεν τὸν λαὸν τοῦ ἀρχιερέως ____________________

2. While you are coming to know (γινώσκω = come to know) these things we shall come into the city.

ὑμῶν ταῦτα ____________________ ἐλευσόμεθα εἰς τὴν πόλιν.

3. While the Lord was establishing his covenant with us, Peter spoke these things to the disciples.

ταῦτα τοῖς μαθηταῖς ἐλάλει ὁ Πέτρος τοῦ κυρίου ______________
τὴν διαθήκην αὐτοῦ πρὸς ἡμᾶς.

4. We were in the city while the people were being led astray.

   ἐν τῇ πόλει ἦμεν τοῦ λαοῦ ______________________________

5. While these things were being spoken the Lord established his covenant with us.

   τούτων ____________________ ὁ κύριος ἔστησεν τὴν διαθήκην αὐτοῦ πρὸς ἡμᾶς.

6. While she was in the city the chief priest was leading the people astray.

   ἐν τῇ πόλει ____________ αὐτῆς ἐπλάνα τὸν λαὸν ὁ ἀρχιερεύς.

7. While the widows were speaking to the apostles we were in the city.

   τῶν χηρῶν ________________ τοῖς ἀποστόλοις ἦμεν ἐν τῇ πόλει.

8. While I was coming to know these things the people were being led astray.

   ἐμοῦ ταῦτα ____________________ ὁ λαὸς ἐπλανᾶτο.

Exercises to Lesson Thirty

Exercise 30-A: Give the future active participle of each of the following verbs, in the gender, number, and case required (imitate the model; review Pars. 91-94, 177, and 201 for the future stem):

Model: λύω	masc. sg. nom.	λύσων
1. ποιέω (ποιῶ)	" " dat.	________
2. δίδωμι	" pl. nom.	________
3. γράφω	fem. sg. nom.	________
4. ἀκούω	" " gen.	________
5. ζητέω (ζητῶ)	neut. sg. nom.	________
6. βαπτίζω	" " gen.	________
7. ἵστημι	" " dat.	________
8. τίθημι	fem. pl. nom.	________
9. ἀγαπάω (ἀγαπῶ)	" " gen.	________
10. ἄγω	" " dat.	________

Exercise 30-B: Give the future middle participle for each of the following verbs, in the gender, number, and case required:

1. παύω	masc. sg. nom.	________
2. λούω	" pl. acc.	________
3. νίπτω	fem. sg. dat.	________
4. βαπτίζω	" pl. gen.	________
5. τίθημι	neut. pl. nom.	________

Exercise 30-C: Give the future passive participle for each of the following verbs, in the gender, number, and case required (see Pars. 126f, 134-136):

1. βαπτίζω	masc. sg. nom.	______
2. λαλέω (λαλῶ)	" pl. gen.	______
3. ἀγαπάω (ἀγαπῶ)	fem. sg. nom.	______
4. πληρόω (πληρῶ)	neut. pl. acc.	______

Exercise 30-D: Complete the Greek sentences below so that they will correctly render the English sentences above them. Be guided by the models provided.

Model (a): The prophet is coming to baptize the disciples.
ὁ προφήτης ἔρχεται βαπτίσων τοὺς μαθητάς.

Model (b): The disciples who are about to be baptized are glorifying God.
οἱ μαθηταὶ οἱ βαπτισθησόμενοι δοξάζουσιν τὸν θεόν.

Model (c): We shall receive the body which is to be.
λημψόμεθα τὸ σῶμα τὸ γενησόμενον.

1. The prophets are coming to baptize the disciples.
οἱ προφῆται ἔρχονται ______

2. She is coming to baptize the child.
ἔρχεται ______ τὸ παιδίον.

3. She is coming to be baptized.
ἔρχεται ______

4. We shall see the city which is to be.
ὀψόμεθα τὴν πόλιν ______

5. We know the prophet who is about to baptize the disciples.

γινώσκομεν τὸν προφήτην ______________________________

6. You are coming with the ones who are about to baptize you.

ἔρχεσθε σὺν ______________________________

7. You are coming with the ones who are about to be baptized.

ἔρχεσθε μετὰ ______________________________

8. We glorify God as we are about to be baptized.

δοξάζομεν τὸν θεὸν ______________________________

Exercises to Lesson Thirty-One

Exercise 31-A: Give the aorist active participle for each of the following verbs, in the gender, number, and case required. Remember that aorist participles do not have the augment.

Note: Some of the verbs in this list are μι-verbs, and some have second aorists. (Check Appendix II, if necessary.)

Model: λύω	masc. sg. nom.	λύσας
1. πέμπω	" " gen.	________
2. λείπω (cf. §244)	" " dat.	________
3. ἄγω (cf. §244)	" " acc.	________
4. διώκω	" pl. nom.	________
5. δίδωμι	" " gen.	________
6. εὑρίσκω (cf. §95)	" " dat.	________
7. κηρύσσω	" " acc.	________
8. τίθημι	fem. sg. nom.	________
9. ποιέω (ποιῶ)	" " gen.	________
10. λέγω (cf. §244)	" " dat.	________
11. ἀγαπάω (ἀγαπῶ)	" " acc.	________
12. πληρόω (πληρῶ)	" pl. nom.	________
13. ἐλέγχω	" " gen.	________
14. γράφω	" " dat.	________
15. λαλέω (λαλῶ)	" " acc.	________
16. ζητέω (ζητῶ)	neut. sg. nom.	________
17. ὁράω (ὁρῶ) (cf. §244)	" " gen.	________
18. ἀκούω	" " dat.	________
19. πιστεύω	neut. pl. nom.	________
20. βαπτίζω	" " dat.	________

Exercise 31-B: Give the aorist passive participle for each of the following verbs, in the gender, number, and case required. Remember that aorist participles do not have the augment.

Note: Some of the verbs in this list are μι -verbs, and some have second aorists passive.

Model: λύω	masc.	sg.	nom.	λυθείς
1. πέμπω	"	"	dat.	______
2. λέγω	"	"	acc.	______
3. ἄγω	"	pl.	gen.	______
4. διώκω	"	"	acc.	______
5. εὑρίσκω	fem.	sg.	nom.	______
6. κηρύσσω	"	"	gen.	______
7. τίθημι	"	pl.	nom.	______
8. ποιέω (ποιῶ)	"	"	gen.	______
9. δίδωμι	"	"	dat.	______
10. ἵστημι	neut.	sg.	nom.	______
11. ἀγαπάω (ἀγαπῶ)	"	"	gen.	______
12. πληρόω (πληρῶ)	"	"	dat.	______
13. ἐλέγχω	"	"	acc.	______
14. γράφω	"	pl.	nom.	______
15. λαλέω (λαλῶ)	"	"	gen.	______
16. ζητέω (ζητῶ)	"	"	dat.	______
17. ὁράω (ὁρῶ)	"	"	acc.	______
18. ἀκούω	neut.	pl.	dat.	______
19. πιστεύω	masc.	"	dat.	______
20. βαπτίζω	fem.	"	dat.	______

Exercise 31-C: Complete the Greek sentences below so that they will correctly render the English sentences above them. Be guided by the models provided:

Model (a): Those who heard his words believe in him.
οἱ ἀκούσαντες τοὺς λόγους αὐτοῦ πιστεύουσιν εἰς αὐτόν.

Model (b): After we had heard his words we believed in him.
ἀκούσαντες τοὺς λόγους αὐτοῦ ἐπιστεύσαμεν εἰς αὐτόν.

Model (c): After we had heard his words, the disciples went into the city.
ἡμῶν ἀκουσάντων τοὺς λόγους αὐτοῦ οἱ μαθηταὶ ἐπορεύθησαν εἰς τὴν πόλιν.

1. The disciples who had heard his words went into the city.
_______________ ἐπορεύθησαν εἰς τὴν πόλιν.

2. After the disciples had heard his words, we went into the city.
_______________ ἐπορεύθημεν εἰς τὴν πόλιν.

3. Because we had believed in him we heard his words.
_______________ ἠκούσαμεν τοὺς λόγους αὐτοῦ.

4. Because she had heard his words she believed in him.
_______________ ἐπίστευσεν εἰς αὐτόν.

5. After she had heard his words, we went into the city.
_______________ ἐπορεύθημεν εἰς τὴν πόλιν.

6. Those who have believed in him will hear his words.
_______________ ἀκούσουσιν τοὺς λόγους αὐτοῦ.

7. When I have heard his words I shall go into the city.
_______________ πορεύσομαι εἰς τὴν πόλιν.

8. After I heard his words, you went into the city.
_______________ ἐπορεύθης εἰς τὴν πόλιν.

Exercise 31-D: Complete the Greek sentences below so that they will correctly render the English sentences above them. Be guided by the models provided.

Model (a): He who said these things is coming out of the house.
ὁ εἰπὼν ταῦτα ἔρχεται ἐκ τοῦ οἴκου.

Model (b): When we had seen the Lord, we came out of the house.
ἰδόντες τὸν κύριον ἤλθομεν ἐκ τοῦ οἴκου.

Model (c): When he had come out of the house, we saw the disciples.
ἐλθόντος αὐτοῦ ἐκ τοῦ οἴκου, εἴδομεν τοὺς μαθητάς.

1. Those who saw the Lord are coming out of the house.
   ______________________________ ἔρχονται ἐκ τοῦ οἴκου.

2. Those who came out of the house will see the Lord.
   ______________________________ ὄψονται τὸν κύριον.

3. After we said these things we came out of the house.
   ______________________________ ἤλθομεν ἐκ τοῦ οἴκου.

4. When she had said these things she came out of the house.
   ________________________ ἦλθεν ἐκ τοῦ οἴκου.

5. We have seen the Lord who said these things.
   εἴδομεν τὸν κύριον ______________________________

6. We know the man who came out of the house.
   γινώσκομεν τὸν ἄνδρα ______________________________

7. He came out of the house of the one who had seen the Lord.
   ἦλθεν ἐκ τοῦ οἴκου ______________________________

8. He came with the one who had said these things.
   ἦλθεν σὺν ______________________________

Exercise 31-E: Complete the Greek sentences below so that they will correctly render the English sentences above them. Be guided by the models provided:

Model (a): After he had given them the bread, he gave them the cup.

δοὺς αὐτοῖς τὸν ἄρτον, τὸ ποτήριον αὐτοῖς ἔδωκεν.

Model (b): He who laid down his life for us will establish a new covenant with us.

ὁ ὑπὲρ ἡμῶν θεὶς τὴν ψυχὴν αὐτοῦ στήσει καινὴν διαθήκην πρὸς ἡμᾶς.

Model (c): When God had established the covenant with the Jews, Moses took his stand upon the mountain.

στήσαντος τοῦ θεοῦ τὴν διαθήκην πρὸς τοὺς Ἰουδαίους, Μωϋσῆς ἔστη ἐπὶ τοῦ ὄρους.

(Remember that ἵστημι (a) in its transitive forms means establish, cause to stand, but (b) in its intransitive forms means stand, stand firm, take a stand. Review Par. 204.)

1. He who gave us the bread will give us the cup.

   ______________________________ δώσει ἡμῖν τὸ ποτήριον.

2. We will give the cup to the one who gave us the bread.

   δώσομεν τὸ ποτήριον ______________________________

3. Having taken his stand upon the mountain, Moses gave the law to the people.

   ______________________________ Μωϋσῆς τὸν νόμον τῷ λαῷ ἔδωκεν.

4. God will save her because she laid down her life for the child.

   ὁ θεὸς σώσει αὐτὴν ______________________ ὑπὲρ τοῦ παιδίου.

5. The disciples give glory to him who laid down his life for them.

   οἱ μαθηταὶ δόξαν διδόασιν ______________________ ὑπὲρ αὐτῶν.

6. Those who stood upon the mountain will be made to stand in the presence of God.

   ______________________________ σταθήσονται ἔμπροσθεν θεοῦ.

Exercise 31-F: Complete the Greek sentences below so that they will correctly render the English sentences above them. Be guided by the models provided:

Model (a): When it was day, that which had been spoken by the prophet was fulfilled.

ἡμέρας γενομένης τὸ λαληθὲν ὑπὸ τοῦ προφήτου ἐπληρώθη.

Model (b): That which had been said by the Lord will be spoken through the prophets.

τὸ ῥηθὲν ὑπὸ τοῦ κυρίου λαληθήσεται διὰ τῶν προφητῶν.

Model (c): These words were said by the Lord to those who had been loved by him.

οὗτοι οἱ λόγοι ἐρρήθησαν ὑπὸ τοῦ κυρίου τοῖς ἀγαπηθεῖσιν ὑπ' αὐτοῦ.

1. When it was Sabbath, these words were spoken.

 ________________ τοῦ σαββάτου, οἱ λόγοι οὗτοι ἐλαλήθησαν.

2. When these things had been said, the prophet spoke to the Lord.

 ______________________________ ἐλάλησεν τῷ κυρίῳ ὁ προφήτης.

3. The commandment which was spoken by the Lord has been fulfilled.

 ἐπληρώθη ἡ ἐντολὴ ______________________ ὑπὸ τοῦ κυρίου.

4. The laws which have been fulfilled were given to us by the Lord.

 ἡμῖν ὑπὸ τοῦ κυρίου ἐδόθησαν οἱ νόμοι ____________________

5. We who have been loved by the Lord love our brethren.

 τοὺς ἀδελφοὺς ἡμῶν ἀγαπῶμεν οἱ ὑπὸ τοῦ κυρίου ______________

6. These things were said to him who was loved by the Lord.

 ἐρρήθησαν ταῦτα ________________________ ὑπὸ τοῦ κυρίου.

Exercises to Lesson Thirty-Two

Exercise 32-A: Give (1) the present and (2) aorist active infinitives, (3) the present middle or passive infinitives, and (4) the aorist passive infinitive for each of the following verbs. (Refer, if necessary, to Pars. 95(3)-(7), 126-131.) Second aorists are marked (2).

	Present Active Infinitive	Aorist Active Infinitive	Present Midd. or Pass. Infinitive	Aorist Passive Infinitive
Model: λύω	λύειν	λῦσαι	λύεσθαι	λυθῆναι
1. πέμπω	______	______	______	______
2. γράφω	______	______	______	(2) ______
3. διώκω	______	______	______	______
4. κηρύσσω	______	______	______	______
5. βαπτίζω	______	______	______	______
6. εὑρίσκω	______	(2) ______	______	______
7. λαμβάνω	______	(2) ______	______	______
8. βάλλω	______	(2) ______	______	______
9. κρύπτω	______	______	______	(2) ______
10. ποιέω	______	______	______	______
11. τιμάω	______	______	______	______
12. ἵστημι	______	(1) ______	______	______
		(2) ______		
13. τίθημι	______	______	______	______
14. δίδωμι	______	______	______	______
15. δράω	______	(2) ______	______	______

16. λέγω ____________ (2)____________ ____________ ____________

17. λαλέω ____________ ____________ ____________ ____________

18. ζητέω ____________ ____________ ____________ ____________

19. πληρόω ____________ ____________ ____________ ____________

Exercise 32-B: Study the models given below, and then translate the numbered sentences below them into English:

Model:

(a)	δύνασαι τέκνον θεοῦ γενέσθαι.	You can become a child of God.
(b)	θέλω σε πιστὸν εἶναι.	I want you to be faithful.
(c)	ὁ υἱὸς τοῦ ἀνθρώπου μέλλει ἔρχεσθαι εἰς τὸν κόσμον.	The Son of Man is about to come into the world.
(d)	ὁ ἀνὴρ ὀφείλει τὴν ἀλήθειαν τῷ ἀδελφῷ λέγειν.	The man ought to tell the truth to the brother.
(e)	ὁ ἀπόστολος βούλεται μαθητὰς ἔχειν.	The apostle wants to have disciples.
(f)	ζητοῦμεν ποιῆσαι τὰ ἔργα τοῦ πατρὸς ἡμῶν.	We are seeking to do the works of our father.

1. ἠδύναντο τέκνα θεοῦ γενέσθαι.

____

2. θέλουσιν ἡμᾶς πιστοὺς εἶναι.

____

3. οἱ ἄνδρες ἤμελλον τὴν ἀλήθειαν τοῖς ἀδελφοῖς αὐτῶν λέγειν.

____

4. βούλει ἔρχεσθαι εἰς τὸν κόσμον.

___

5. ζητήσω ποιῆσαι τὰ ἔργα μου.

___

6. ὀφείλομεν μαθητὰς ἔχειν.

___

7. δυνησόμεθα λέγειν τὴν ἀλήθειαν τοῖς ἀδελφοῖς ἡμῶν.

___

8. ἤθελον ἐγὼ αὐτοὺς ποιῆσαι τὰ ἔργα μου.

___

9. ἠθέλησα ποιῆσαι τὰ ἔργα μου.

___

10. ἐζήτουν οἱ ἀπόστολοι μαθητὰς ἔχειν.

___

Exercise 32-C: Refer to the models provided for Exercise 32-B, and translate the following sentences into Greek:

1. We are able to have disciples.

___

2. The man wishes to do the works of his father.

___

3. We used to be able to tell the truth to our brothers. (See Par.96)

___

4. We have wanted the apostle to have disciples. (See Par.96)

___

5. The man was seeking to be faithful.

___

6. The apostle was obliged to have disciples.

____

7. We have been able to do our works.

____

8. You will be able to become a child of God.

____

9. You will want us to tell the truth to them.

____

10. God wants us to become his children.

____

<u>Exercise 32-D</u>: Study the models given below, and then translate the numbered sentences below them into English:

<u>Model</u>:

(a) ὁ πατὴρ ἀκούει τὴν φωνὴν τοῦ υἱοῦ αὐτοῦ.	The father hears the voice of his son.
(b) ὁ προφήτης δίδωσι νόμους τῷ λαῷ.	The prophet gives laws to the people.
(c) λαλοῦμεν ὑμῖν ἐν τῷ ὀνόματι τοῦ κυρίου.	We are speaking to you in the name of the Lord.
(d) ὁ θεὸς ἵστησιν τὴν διαθήκην αὐτοῦ πρὸς ἡμᾶς.	God is establishing his covenant with us.
(e) τὰ ἔθνη ἔλαβον τοὺς λόγους τοῦ ἀγγέλου.	The gentiles received the words of the angel.

1. ὁ πατὴρ θέλει τὴν φωνὴν τοῦ υἱοῦ αὐτοῦ ἀκοῦσαι.

____

2. ὁ προφήτης μέλλει νόμους τῷ λαῷ διδόναι.

____

3. ὀφείλομεν ὑμῖν λαλεῖν ἐν τῷ ὀνόματι τοῦ θεοῦ.

____

4. ὁ θεὸς βούλεται τὴν διαθήκην αὐτοῦ στῆσαι πρὸς ἡμᾶς.

____

5. ζητεῖ τὰ ἔθνη τοὺς λόγους τοῦ ἀγγέλου λαβεῖν.

____

<u>Exercise 32-E</u>: Referring to the models above, translate the following sentences into Greek:

---

1. The son ought to hear the voice of his father.

____

2. The prophet sought to give laws to the people.

____

3. You will be able to speak to us in the name of the Lord.

____

4. The gentiles wish to hear the words of the angel.

____

Exercise 32-F: Study the models given below, and then translate the numbered sentences below them into English:

Model:

(a) πιστεύει ὁ βασιλεὺς εἰς τὸν θεόν.	The king believes in God.
(b) ταῖς ἐκκλησίαις γράφει ὁ ἀπόστολος.	The apostle is writing to the churches.
(c) πορεύεται ὁ ἀρχιερεὺς εἰς τὴν πόλιν.	The chief priest is going into the city.
(d) τὰ παιδία αὐτῆς ἀγαπᾷ ἡ μήτηρ.	The mother loves her children.
(e) ὁ ποιμὴν τὴν ψυχὴν αὐτοῦ τίθησιν ὑπὲρ τῶν προβάτων.	The shepherd lays down his life for the sheep.
(f) καλεῖ αὐτοὺς ὁ διδάσκαλος.	The teacher is calling them.

1. ἐζήτει ὁ βασιλεὺς εἰς τὸν θεὸν πιστεύειν.

____

2. μέλλει ὁ ἀπόστολος ταῖς ἐκκλησίαις γράφειν.

____

3. δύναται ὁ ἀρχιερεὺς εἰς τὴν πόλιν πορεύεσθαι.

____

4. ὀφείλει ἡ μήτηρ τὰ παιδία αὐτῆς ἀγαπᾶν.

____

5. ἤθελεν ὁ διδάσκαλος αὐτοὺς καλέσαι.

____

Exercise 32-G: Refer to the models above, and translate the following sentences into Greek:

1. The shepherd ought to lay down his life for the sheep.

____

2. We want the teacher to call them.

____

3. The chief priest is about to go into the city.

____

4. The children ought to love their mother.

____

Exercises to Lesson Thirty-Three

Exercise 33-A: Refer to (a), (b), and (c) below, and translate the numbered sentences beneath them into Greek:

(a) ἔστησεν ὁ θεὸς τὴν διαθήκην. God established the covenant.

(b) ὁ κύριος βαπτίζει τοὺς μαθητάς. The Lord is baptizing the disciples.

(c) ἡμᾶς ἀγαπᾷ ὁ θεός. God loves us.

1. God must establish the covenant (= It is necessary for God to establish the covenant).

   ____

2. The covenant had to be established.

   ____

3. It is lawful for the disciples to be baptized. (Use a present inf.)

   ____

4. We need to be baptized. (Use aorist infinitive.)

   ____

5. God is worthy to be loved.

   ____

6. We must love the Lord.

   ____

7. God loved us before we loved him.

   ____

8. God has power to establish the covenant.

   ____

9. This is God's will, for us to baptize disciples.

   ____

10. The disciples are worthy to be baptized.

   ____

Exercise 33-B: Refer to (a), (b), and (c) below, and translate the numbered sentences beneath them into English:

(a) δίδωσιν ἡμῖν τοὺς ἄρτους. He gives us the loaves.

(b) πιστεύομεν εἰς αὐτόν. We believe in him.

(c) ἀκούομεν τοὺς λόγους αὐτοῦ. We hear his words.

1. ἐν τῷ ἡμῖν διδόναι αὐτὸν τοὺς ἄρτους ἠκούομεν τοὺς λόγους αὐτοῦ.

____

2. μετὰ τὸ ἀκοῦσαι τοὺς λόγους αὐτοῦ, ἐπιστεύσαμεν εἰς αὐτόν.

____

3. διὰ τὸ ἀκούειν τοὺς λόγους αὐτοῦ, πιστεύσομεν εἰς αὐτόν.

____

4. πρὸ τοῦ πιστεῦσαι εἰς αὐτὸν ἠκούσαμεν τοὺς λόγους αὐτοῦ.

____

5. πιστεύσομεν εἰς αὐτὸν εἰς τὸ ἡμῖν δοῦναι αὐτὸν τοὺς ἄρτους.

____

6. ἔδωκεν ἡμῖν τοὺς ἄρτους ὥστε ἀκοῦσαι ἡμᾶς τοὺς λόγους αὐτοῦ.

____

7. ἠκούομεν τοὺς λόγους αὐτοῦ τοῦ πιστεύειν εἰς αὐτόν.

____

8. ἐπιστεύσαμεν εἰς αὐτὸν ἕως τοῦ ἀκοῦσαι τοὺς λόγους αὐτοῦ.

____

9. δίδωσιν ἡμῖν τοὺς ἄρτους πρὸς τὸ ἡμᾶς πιστεύειν εἰς αὐτόν.

____

10. ἐν τῷ ἡμᾶς τοὺς λόγους αὐτοῦ ἀκούειν ἐδίδου ἡμῖν τοὺς ἄρτους.

____

Exercises to Lesson Thirty-Four

Exercise 34-A: Following the rule given in Par. 265, form adverbs from the following adjectives, and give their meanings (imitate the model):

	Adjective		Adverb
Model:	ἀκριβής,	strict (m.gen.pl. ἀκριβῶν)	ἀκριβῶς, strictly
1.	ἄξιος,	worthy	________
2.	ἀσφαλής,	safe (see Par. 163(iii))	________
3.	δίκαιος,	righteous	________
4.	εὐσεβής,	pious (see Par. 163(iii)).	________
5.	εὐθύς,	straight, direct (see Par. 161)	________
6.	φανερός,	manifest, plain	________
7.	καλός,	good	________
8.	ὀρθός,	straight, right	________
9.	ἄφρων,	foolish (see Par. 158(ii))	________
10.	ὅμοιος,	similar, like	________

Exercise 34-B: Consult the lists in Pars. 265ff and supply the Greek equivalents for the English adverbs given in the table below (a few forms not in the lists have already been supplied):

1.	how?	when?	where?	whence?
	________	________	________	________
2.	somehow	at some time	somewhere	(from somewhere)
	πώς	________	________	(ποθέν)

3.	(in that way) (ἐκείνως)	then	there	thence
4.	thus	now(any equivalent)	here	hence
5.	as, how ὡς; ὅπως	when (2 forms)	where (2 forms)	whence

Exercise 34-C: Referring to the lists in Pars. 265-67 for vocabulary, supply the missing words so that the Greek sentences will translate the English sentences above them:

1. Again he spoke to them in parables.
   ______ εἶπεν ἐν παραβολαῖς αὐτοῖς.
2. I always taught in the synagogue.
   ἐγὼ ______ ἐδίδαξα ἐν συναγωγῇ.
3. Then they will see the Son of Man coming.
   ______ ὄψονται τὸν υἱὸν τοῦ ἀνθρώπου ἐρχόμενον.
4. You must be born from above.
   δεῖ ὑμᾶς γεννηθῆναι ______
5. This is indeed the saviour of the world.
   οὗτός ἐστιν ______ ὁ σωτὴρ τοῦ κόσμου.
6. My daughter has just now died.
   ἡ θυγάτηρ μου ______ ἐτελεύτησεν.
7. I am there in the midst of them.
   ______ εἰμι ἐν μέσῳ αὐτῶν.

8. From there he came into the house.

_____________ ἦλθεν εἰς οἰκίαν.

9. Perfect love casts out fear.

ἡ τελεία ἀγάπη ________ βάλλει τὸν φόβον.

10. Afterwards I went into the regions of Syria.

______________ ἦλθον εἰς τὰ κλίματα τῆς Συρίας.

11. You are still in your sins.

_____________ ἐστὲ ἐν ταῖς ἁμαρτίαις ὑμῶν.

12. Immediately the cock crowed.

_____________ ἀλέκτωρ ἐφώνησεν.

13. The true light already shines.

τὸ φῶς τὸ ἀληθινὸν ________ φαίνει.

14. They persecuted the prophets thus.

____________ ἐδίωξαν τοὺς προφήτας.

15. Elijah must come first.

'Ηλίαν δεῖ ἐλθεῖν ______________

16. You will be with me in paradise today.

______________ μετ' ἐμοῦ ἔσῃ ἐν τῷ παραδείσῳ.

17. It is good for us to be here.

καλόν ἐστιν ἡμᾶς __________ εἶναι.

18. My time is near.

ὁ καιρός μου __________ ἐστιν.

19. The Jerusalem which is above is free.

ἡ __________ 'Ιερουσαλὴμ ἐλευθέρα ἐστίν.

20. You will really be free.

________________ ἐλεύθεροι ἔσεσθε.

21. In the morning the chief priests took counsel against him.

    _____________ συμβούλιον ἔλαβον οἱ ἀρχιερεῖς κατ᾽αὐτοῦ.

22. Tomorrow we shall go into the city.

    ___________ πορευσόμεθα εἰς τὴν πόλιν.

23. Nevertheless I say to you, come after me.

    ___________ λέγω ὑμῖν, δεῦτε ὀπίσω μου.

24. When they heard, the disciples were exceedingly afraid.

    ἀκούσαντες οἱ μαθηταὶ ἐφοβήθησαν _____________

25. We are justified freely, by his grace.

    δικαιούμεθα _____________ τῇ αὐτοῦ χάριτι.

Exercises to Lesson Thirty-Five

Exercise 35-A: Each of the sentences below may be translated in four different ways; one way is given in each case: supply the other three (imitate the model):

Model: The teacher is greater than his disciple.

(a) ὁ διδάσκαλος μείζων ἐστὶν ἢ ὁ μαθητὴς αὐτοῦ.

(b) ὁ διδάσκαλος μείζων τοῦ μαθητοῦ αὐτοῦ ἐστιν.

(c) ὁ διδάσκαλος μείζων ἐστὶν παρὰ τὸν μαθητὴν αὐτοῦ.

(d) ὁ διδάσκαλος μείζων ἐστὶν ὑπὲρ τὸν μαθητὴν αὐτοῦ.

1. We have been cleansed by a better sacrifice than this.

(a) ____

(b) ____

(c) ἐκαθαρίσθημεν θυσίᾳ κρείσσονι παρὰ ταύτην.

(d) ____

2. The sect of the Pharisees is stricter than that of the Sadducees.

(a) ἡ αἵρεσις τῶν Φαρισαίων ἀκριβεστέρα ἐστὶν ἢ ἡ τῶν Σαδδουκαίων.

(b) ____

(c) ____

(d) ____

3. He loved the darkness rather than the light.

(a) ____

(b) ἠγάπησεν τὴν σκοτίαν μᾶλλον τοῦ φωτός.

(c) ____

(d) ____

4. It will be more tolerable for us than for you.

(a) ____________________

(b) ____________________

(c) ____________________

(d) ἡμῖν ἔσται ἀνεκτότερον ὑπὲρ ὑμᾶς.

Exercises to Lesson Thirty-Six

Exercise 36-A: Supply the correct form of μέγας in each Greek sentence so that it will correctly translate the English sentence above it:

1. This one shall be called great in the kingdom of heaven.
   οὗτος ____________ κληθήσεται ἐν τῇ βασιλείᾳ τῶν οὐρανῶν.
2. This is the great commandment.
   αὕτη ἐστὶν ἡ ______________ ἐντολή.
3. Jesus cried out with a great voice.
   ἐβόησεν ὁ Ἰησοῦς φωνῇ ______________ (ἡ φωνή)
4. He is doing great signs.
   ποιεῖ σημεῖα ______________
5. This mystery is great.
   τὸ μυστήριον τοῦτο ___________ ἐστίν.
6. We have a great high priest.
   ἔχομεν ἀρχιερέα ______________
7. We have heard the voice of a great prophet.
   ἠκούσαμεν τὴν φωνὴν προφήτου ______________
8. The Gentiles will be judged by the great angels.
   τὰ ἔθνη κριθήσεται ὑπὸ τῶν ἀγγέλων τῶν ________________
9. He will make your sons great among the Gentiles.
   ποιήσει τοὺς υἱοὺς ὑμῶν ________________ ἐν τοῖς ἔθνεσιν.
10. The king went out of the great city.
    ὁ βασιλεὺς ἐπορεύθη ἐκ τῆς πόλεως τῆς _________________

Exercise 36-B: Supply the correct form of πολύς so that the Greek sentences will correctly translate the English ones:

1. Great is your reward in heaven.
   ὁ μισθὸς ὑμῶν ____________ ἐν τοῖς οὐρανοῖς.

2. They went into many towns of the Samaritans.
   εἰς ______________ κώμας τῶν Σαμαριτῶν ἐπορεύθησαν. (ἡ κώμη)

3. He saw a great multitude.
   εἶδεν ___________ ὄχλον. (ὁ ὄχλος)

4. He healed many men.
   ἄνδρας ______________ ἐθεράπευσεν. (ὁ ἀνήρ)

5. I will make you a father of many nations.
   πατέρα ______________ ἐθνῶν θήσω σε.

6. Many shall come in my name.
   _____________ ἐλεύσονται ἐπὶ τῷ ὀνόματί μου.

7. I have much boldness in Christ.
   ______________ παρρησίαν ἐν Χριστῷ ἔχω.

8. When much discussion took place, Peter spoke.
   _____________ ζητήσεως γενομένης, ἐλάλησεν ὁ Πέτρος.

9. They honored us with many honors.
   ______________ τιμαῖς ἐτίμησαν ἡμᾶς.

10. He was teaching them many things in parables.
    ἐδίδασκεν αὐτοὺς ἐν παραβολαῖς _____________

11. There were many women there.
    ἦσαν ἐκεῖ γυναῖκες _____________

12. I heard a voice of many waters.
    ἤκουσα φωνὴν ὑδάτων ______________

Exercise 36-C: Supply the proper forms of the adjectives required so that the Greek sentences will correctly render the English ones:

1. He was writing with ink.
   ἔγραφεν τῷ ______________
2. He will lead us out of the black darkness.
   ἄξει ἡμᾶς ἐκ τῆς ______________ σκοτίας.
3. He is leading you into the black darkness.
   ἄγει ὑμᾶς εἰς τὸ ______________ σκότος.
4. He will have double honor.
   ἕξει τιμὴν ______________
5. He will receive a fourfold reward.
   λήμψεται μισθὸν ______________ (ὁ μισθός)
6. The king sits upon a golden throne.
   καθίζει ὁ βασιλεὺς ἐπὶ θρόνον ______________ (ὁ θρόνος)
7. The soldiers are wearing iron breastplates.
   οἱ στρατιῶται φοροῦσιν θώρακας ______________ (ὁ θώραξ)
8. The high priest has the silver vessels.
   ὁ ἀρχιερεὺς ἔχει τὰ σκεύη τὰ ______________
9. The Lord is wearing a purple garment.
   φωρεῖ ὁ κύριος ἱμάτιον ______________ (τὸ ἱμάτιον)
10. The gate of the city is bronze.
   ______________ ἡ πύλη τῆς πόλεως.

Exercise 36-D: Supply the proper form of πᾶς, together with the proper form of the article, if necessary, in each Greek sentence so that it will correctly translate the English sentence above it:

1. I will give you all the kingdoms of the world.

   δώσω σοι ______________________ βασιλείας τοῦ κόσμου.

2. All the prophets prophesied until John.

   ____________________ προφῆται ἕως 'Ιωάννου ἐπροφήτευσαν.

3. He healed them all.

   ἐθεράπευσεν αὐτοὺς ______________

4. He spoke all these things in parables.

   ταῦτα ______________ ἐλάλησεν ἐν παραβολαῖς.

5. All of you are brothers.

   ______________ ὑμεῖς ἀδελφοί ἐστε.

6. Everyone who does sin is a slave of sin.

   _____________ ποιῶν τὴν ἁμαρτίαν δοῦλός ἐστιν τῆς ἁμαρτίας.

7. All those who believe in him shall have eternal life.

   _________________ πιστεύοντες εἰς αὐτὸν ἕξουσιν ζωὴν αἰώνιον.

8. The Lord will deliver me from every evil work.

   ῥύσεταί με ὁ κύριος ἀπὸ ______________ ἔργου πονηροῦ.

9. Every eye will see him.

   ὄψεται αὐτὸν ____________ ὀφθαλμός.

10. The Lord has made him heir of all things.

    ὁ κύριος αὐτὸν ἔθηκεν κληρονόμον ___________________

Exercise 36-E: Supply the proper form of ὅλος in each Greek sentence so that it will correctly render the English sentence above it:

1. You shall love the Lord your God with all your heart.

   ἀγαπήσεις Κύριον τὸν θεόν σου ἐν ____________ τῇ καρδίᾳ σου.

2. He has gained the whole world.

   ἐκέρδησεν τὸν κόσμον ______________

3. Satan deceives the whole of mankind (= the whole inhabited world).

   ὁ Σατανᾶς πλανᾷ τὴν οἰκουμένην ______________

4. A little leaven leavens the whole lump.

   μικρὰ ζύμη ______________ τὸ φύραμα ζυμοῖ.

5. For your sake we are being put to death all day.

   ἕνεκέν σου θανατούμεθα ______________ τὴν ἡμέραν.

<u>Exercise 36-F</u>: Supply the proper form of ἕκαστος in each Greek sentence so that it will correctly render the English sentence above it:

1. They made four parts, a part for each soldier.

   ἐποίησαν τέσσερα μέρη ______________ στρατιώτῃ μέρος.

2. Each of you was baptized in the name of Jesus Christ.

   ______________ ὑμῶν ἐβαπτίσθη ἐν ὀνόματι Ἰησοῦ Χριστοῦ.

3. We received gifts from each one of you.

   ἐλάβομεν δῶρα ἀπὸ ______________ ὑμῶν.

4. The work of every one will be made manifest.

   ______________ τὸ ἔργον φανερὸν γενήσεται.

5. Every one is tempted by his own desire.

   ______________ πειράζεται ὑπὸ τῆς ἰδίας ἐπιθυμίας.

Exercises to Lesson Thirty-Seven

Exercise 37-A: Supply the proper form of the required cardinal numeral, so that each Greek sentence will correctly translate the English one above it:

1. These are the names of the twelve apostles.
   τῶν ________________ ἀποστόλων τὰ ὀνόματά ἐστιν ταῦτα.

2. Judas Iscariot was one of the disciples.
   ὁ 'Ιοῦδας ὁ 'Ισκαριώτης ἦν ________ ἐκ τῶν μαθητῶν.

3. Lazarus has two sisters.
   Λάζαρος ἔχει __________ ἀδελφάς.

4. Mary had one sister.
   Μαριὰμ εἶχεν __________ ἀδελφήν.

5. Martha had one brother.
   Μάρθα εἶχεν_______ ἀδελφόν.

6. We have many members in one body.
   ἔχομεν πολλὰ μέλη ἐν _________ σώματι. (τὸ σῶμα)

7. We are members of one body.
   μέλη ἐσμὲν _________ σώματος.

8. I shall give authority to the two angels.
   ἐξουσίαν δώσω τοῖς _________ ἀγγέλοις.

9. A man had three sons.
   ἄνθρωπος εἶχεν __________ υἱοὺς.

10. The Lord gave commandments to the three disciples.
    ἔδωκεν ὁ κύριος ἐντολὰς τοῖς ____________ μαθηταῖς.

Exercise 37-B: Write the Arabic numerals below as Greek numerals, and the Greek numerals as Arabic numerals:

	Arabic	Greek		Greek	Arabic
(a)	536	________	(f)	$\overline{\text{οβ}}$	________
(b)	616	________	(g)	$\overline{\text{ρα}}$	________
(c)	99	________	(h)	$\overline{\text{φκβ}}$	________
(d)	996	________	(i)	$\overline{\text{͵αρνγ}}$	________
(e)	1965	________	(j)	$\overline{\text{ωπη}}$	________

Exercise 37-C: Supply (a) the proper form of ἄλλος and (b) the proper form of ἕτερος so that in either case the Greek sentences will correctly render the English ones:

1. The other disciple loved Jesus.
   ὁ __________ μαθητὴς ἠγάπησεν τὸν 'Ιησοῦν.
   ____

2. The prophet is preaching another gospel.
   ὁ προφήτης κηρύσσει εὐαγγέλιον ______________ (τὸ εὐαγγέλιον)
   ____

3. They went into another city.
   ἐπορεύθησαν εἰς ______________ πόλιν.
   ____

4. Another commandment was given to us.
   ______________ ἐντολὴ ἐδόθη ἡμῖν.
   ____

5. The father gave these things to his other son.
   ὁ πατὴρ ταῦτα ἔδωκεν τῷ ____________ αὐτοῦ υἱῷ.
   ____

Exercises to Lesson Thirty-Eight

Exercise 38-A:

1. The negatives used with verb-forms of the indicative mood are (supply the Greek equivalents):

not ____________

no longer ____________

not yet ____________ or ____________

never ____________

no one ____________

nothing ____________

2. The negatives used with infinitives and participles are:

not ____________

no longer ____________

not yet ____________ or ____________

never ____________

no one ____________

nothing ____________

3. The form οὐκ occurs before ______________________ (consonants, vowels) which have a ______________ (rough, smooth) breathing.

4. The form οὐχ occurs before ______________________ (consonants, vowels) which have a ______________ (rough, smooth) breathing.

5. Οὐ μή with the ______________ indicative expresses a strong negative.

6. Two or more negatives in the same construction ________________ ______________________________ (cancel each other out; reinforce each other).

Exercise 38-B: Supply the appropriate negative in each Greek sentence:

1. I am not the Christ.
   ἐγὼ ________ εἰμὶ ὁ Χριστός.

2. He cannot see the kingdom.
   ________ δύναται ἰδεῖν τὴν βασιλείαν.

3. A lie was not found in their mouth.
   ἐν τῷ στόματι αὐτῶν ________ εὑρέθη ψεῦδος.

4. He who is not with me is against me.
   ὁ ______ ὢν μετ'ἐμοῦ κατ'ἐμοῦ ἐστιν.

5. He who does not honor the son does not honor the father.
   ὁ ________ τιμῶν τὸν υἱὸν ________ τιμᾷ τὸν πατέρα.

6. He who does not love me does not keep my words.
   ὁ ________ ἀγαπῶν με τοὺς λόγους μου _______ τηρεῖ.

7. The Sadducees say that there is no resurrection.
   οἱ Σαδδουκαῖοι λέγουσι _______ εἶναι ἀνάστασιν.

8. You will no longer see my face.
   ______________ ὄψεσθε τὸ πρόσωπόν μου.

9. Since we are no longer under a tutor, we are heirs.
   ______________ ὄντων ἡμῶν ὑπὸ παιδαγωγόν, κληρονόμοι ἐσμέν.

10. No one puts new wine into old wineskins.
    ______________ βάλλει οἶνον νέον εἰς ἀσκοὺς παλαιούς.

11. You never gave me a kid.
    ἐμοὶ ________________ ἔδωκας ἔριφον.

12. They will not hear my voice at all.
    ________________ ἀκούσουσιν τὴν φωνήν μου.

Exercises to Lesson Thirty-Nine

Exercise 39-A: Below are given five Greek sentences with their English translations. Below each Greek sentence are five others, based upon them. Translate these into English. A model is provided.

Model: ἱλαρὸν δότην ἀγαπᾷ ὁ θεός.	God loves a cheerful giver.
(a) μὴ ἱλαρὸν δότην ἀγαπᾷ ὁ θεός;	God doesn't love a cheerful giver, does he?
(b) οὐχ ἱλαρὸν δότην ἀγαπᾷ ὁ θεός;	God does love a cheerful giver, doesn't he?
(c) ποῖον δότην ἀγαπᾷ ὁ θεός;	What kind of giver does God love?
(d) τίνα ἀγαπᾷ ὁ θεός;	Whom does God love?
(e) τίς ἱλαρὸν δότην ἀγαπᾷ;	Who loves a cheerful giver?

1. πᾶν δένδρον ἀγαθὸν καρποὺς καλοὺς ποιεῖ. — Every good tree bears good fruit.

(a) μὴ πᾶν δένδρον ἀγαθὸν καρποὺς καλοὺς ποιεῖ; ____________________

(b) οὐ πᾶν δένδρον ἀγαθὸν καρποὺς καλοὺς ποιεῖ; ____________________

(c) τί καλοὺς καρποὺς ποιεῖ; ____________________

(d) ποῖον δένδρον καρποὺς καλοὺς ποιεῖ; ____________________

(e) ποίους καρποὺς πᾶν δένδρον ἀγαθὸν ποιεῖ; ____________________

2. οὐκ ἐποίησεν ἐκεῖ δυνάμεις πολλάς. — He did not do many great works there.

(a) μὴ οὐκ ἐποίησεν ἐκεῖ δυνάμεις πολλάς;

(b) τίς οὐκ ἐποίησεν ἐκεῖ δυνάμεις πολλάς;

(c) τί οὐκ ἐποίησεν ἐκεῖ;

(d) ποῦ οὐκ ἐποίησεν δυνάμεις
πολλάς;

(e) πόσας δυνάμεις ἐποίησεν ἐκεῖ;

3. οὐκ ἔστιν ἡ ἀγάπη τοῦ πατρὸς
ἐν αὐτῷ.

The love of the father is not in him.

(a) οὐκ ἔστιν ἡ ἀγάπη τοῦ πατρὸς
ἐν αὐτῷ;

(b) μὴ οὐκ ἔστιν ἡ ἀγάπη τοῦ
πατρὸς ἐν αὐτῷ;

(c) τίνος ἀγάπη οὐκ ἔστιν ἐν
αὐτῷ;

(d) ἐν τίνι ἐστὶν ἡ ἀγάπη τοῦ
πατρός;

(e) ποία ἀγάπη ἐστὶν ἐν αὐτῷ;

4. ἔδωκεν αὐτοῖς ἐξουσίαν τέκνα θεοῦ γενέσθαι.

He gave them power to become children of God.

(a) τίσιν ἔδωκεν ἐξουσίαν;

____

____

(b) τί ἔδωκεν αὐτοῖς;

____

(c) ποίαν ἐξουσίαν ἔδωκεν αὐτοῖς;

____

____

(d) τίνος τέκνα ἔδωκεν αὐτοῖς ἐξουσίαν γενέσθαι;

____

____

(e) ἔδωκεν αὐτοῖς ἐξουσίαν τέκνα θεοῦ γενέσθαι;

____

____

5. ὁ δοῦλος ἐπορεύθη ταχέως ἐκ τοῦ οἴκου.

The slave went quickly out of the house.

(a) τίς ἐπορεύθη ἐκ τοῦ οἴκου;

____

____

(b) πῶς ἐπορεύθη ἐκ τοῦ οἴκου;

____

____

(c) πόθεν ἐπορεύθη ὁ δοῦλος;

____

____

(d) ἐπορεύθη ταχέως ὁ δοῦλος ἐκ τοῦ οἴκου;

____

____

(e) πότε ἐπορεύθη ὁ δοῦλος ἐκ τοῦ οἴκου;

____

____

Exercise 39-B: Same as Exercise 39-A, except that the English sentences are to be translated into Greek.

1. πέμψει ὁ Χριστὸς τοὺς ἀγγέλους αὐτοῦ ἐξ οὐρανοῦ.	Christ will send his angels from heaven.
(a) ______________________	Who will send his angels?
(b) ______________________	Whence will he send them?
(c) ______________________	Whose angels will he send?
(d) ______________________	Whom will Christ send from heaven?
(e) ______________________	Christ will send his angels, won't he?
2. πάντα ἐν ἀληθείᾳ ἐλάλησεν ὑμῖν.	He has spoken all things to you in truth.
(a) ______________________	What things has he spoken to you?
(b) ______________________	How has he spoken all things?
(c) ______________________	To whom has he spoken all things?
(d) ______________________	Who has spoken to you in truth?
(e) ______________________	How many things did he speak to you?

3. ὁ Παῦλος ἅπαξ ἐλιθάσθη ὑπὸ τῶν Ἰουδαίων. — Paul was stoned once by the Jews.

(a) ______________________ Who was stoned?

(b) ______________________ By whom was he stoned?

____

(c) ______________________ How many times was he stoned?

____

(d) ______________________ Paul was not stoned, was he?

____

(e) ______________________ Paul was stoned, wasn't he?

____

4. ἐν ἀρχῇ ἐποίησεν ὁ θεὸς τὰ πάντα ἐν λόγῳ αὐτοῦ. — In the beginning God made everything by his word.

(a) ______________________ When did God make everything?

____

(b) ______________________ How did God make everything?

____

(c) ______________________ Who made everything in the beginning?

____

(d) ______________________ What did God make in the beginning?

____

(e) ______________________ Why did God make everything?

____

5. ὁ σπόρος ἔπεσεν ἐπὶ τὴν γῆν τὴν καλήν.	The seed fell on the good ground.
(a) ____________________ ____________________	What fell on the good ground?
(b) ____________________ ____________________	Where did the seed fall?
(c) ____________________ ____________________	On what kind of ground did it fall?
(d) ____________________ ____________________	How much seed fell on the good ground?
(e) ____________________ ____________________	Which seed fell on the good ground?

Exercise 39-C: Change the direct question to an indirect question introduced as indicated. Imitate the model, paying special attention to changes in person.

Model: τί με λέγετε ἀγαθόν; — Why do you call me good?

ἠρώτησεν αὐτοὺς τί αὐτὸν λέγουσιν ἀγαθόν. — He asked them why they called him good.

1. τὸν νόμον οὐκ ἀκούετε; — Do you not hear the law?

ἠρώτησεν αὐτοὺς ______________ — He asked them whether they did not hear the law.

____

2. σὺ εἶ ὁ βασιλεὺς τῶν Ἰουδαίων; — Are you the king of the Jews?

ἠρώτησεν αὐτὸν ______________ — He asked him whether he was the king of the Jews.

____

3. τί με δεῖ ποιεῖν; — What must I do?

ἠρώτησεν αὐτοὺς ______________ — He asked them what he had to do.

____

4. πῶς σώσω τὴν ψυχήν μου ἐκ θανάτου; — How shall I save my soul from death?

ἠρώτησεν αὐτοὺς ______________ — He asked them how he should save his soul from death.

____

5. τί ζητεῖτε τὸν ζῶντα μετὰ τῶν νεκρῶν; — Why do you seek the living among the dead?

ἠρώτησεν αὐτὰς ______________ — He asked them why they were seeking the living among the dead.

____

____

6. διὰ τί ὁ κόσμος οὐ δύναται ἡμᾶς γινώσκειν;

ἠρώτησαν αὐτὸν ________________

____

Why can the world not know us?

They asked him why the world could not know them.

7. πῶς σταθήσεται ἡ βασιλεία αὐτοῦ;

ἠρώτησαν αὐτὸν ________________

____

How will his kingdom stand?

They asked him how his kingdom would stand.

8. τίνα μαθητὴν βλέπεις;

ἠρώτησέν με ________________

____

Which disciple do you see?

He asked me which disciple I saw.

9. πόσους ἄρτους ἔχετε;

ἠρώτησεν αὐτοὺς ________________

____

How many loaves do you have?

He asked them how many loaves they had.

10. ποῦ ἐστιν ὁ πατήρ σου;

ἠρώτησαν αὐτὸν ________________

____

Where is your father?

They asked him where his father was.

Exercises to Lesson Forty

Exercise 40-A: Supply the correct form of ὅς so that the Greek sentences will correctly translate the English ones (do not assimilate the case of the relative to the case of its antecedent in this Exercise):

1. Who is this who speaks blasphemies?
   τίς ἐστιν οὗτος ______ λαλεῖ βλασφημίας;

2. No one can do the signs that you are doing.
   οὐδεὶς τὰ σημεῖα δύναται ποιεῖν ______ σὺ ποιεῖς.

3. There are six days in which one must work.
   ἓξ ἡμέραι εἰσίν, ἐν ______ δεῖ ἐργάζεσθαι.

4. The bread which I shall give is my flesh.
   ὁ ἄρτος ______ ἐγὼ δώσω ἡ σάρξ μου ἐστίν.

5. He ate the loaves which it is not lawful to eat.
   τοὺς ἄρτους ἔφαγεν ______ οὐκ ἔξεστιν φαγεῖν.

6. What I have, this I give to you.
   ______ ἔχω, τοῦτο σοι δίδωμι.

7. He has justified those whom he called.
   ἐκείνους ἐδικαίωσεν ______ ἐκάλεσεν.

8. This is the church of which I became a minister.
   αὕτη ἐστὶν ἡ ἐκκλησία ______ ἐγενήθην διάκονος.

9. The commandments which we received are good.
   καλαὶ αἱ ἐντολαὶ ______ ἐλάβομεν.

10. These are the apostles through whom we were called.
    οὗτοί εἰσιν οἱ ἀπόστολοι δι' ______ ἐκλήθημεν.

11. We did not see the men with whom you came.
οὐκ εἴδομεν τοὺς ἄνδρας σὺν ________ ἤλθετε.

12. These are words of the truth which sets us free.
οὗτοί εἰσιν λόγοι τῆς ἀληθείας ______ ἡμᾶς ἐλευθεροῖ.

Exercise 40-B: Same directions as for Exercise 40-A, except that in this exercise the relative should be attracted to the case of its antecedent:

1. The father hears the voice of the son whom he sent.
ὁ πατὴρ ἀκούει τὴν φωνὴν τοῦ υἱοῦ _______ ἔπεμψεν.

2. He gave authority to the apostles whom he sent.
ἐξουσίαν ἔδωκεν τοῖς ἀποστόλοις _______ ἔπεμψεν.

3. We are looking for the house of the brothers whom Jesus loved.
ζητοῦμεν τὸν οἶκον τῶν ἀδελφῶν ________ ἠγάπα Ἰησοῦς.

4. Paul preached the gospel among the Gentiles whom the Jews hated.
ἐκήρυξεν Παῦλος τὸ εὐαγγέλιον ἐν τοῖς ἔθνεσιν ________ ἐμίσουν οἱ Ἰουδαῖοι.

5. He called with a great voice which the prophet heard.
ἐφώνησεν φωνῇ μεγάλῃ _______ ἤκουσεν ὁ προφήτης.

6. The nations were saved by the Lord of the church which they persecuted.
τὰ ἔθνη ἐσώθη ὑπὸ τοῦ κυρίου τῆς ἐκκλησίας ________ ἐδίωξεν.

7. These men were working in the vineyard which their father planted.
οὗτοι ἠργάζοντο ἐν τῷ ἀμπελῶνι _______ ἐφύτευσεν ὁ πατὴρ αὐτῶν.

8. God made the world by the word which he spoke.
ἐποίησεν ὁ θεὸς τὸν κόσμον τῷ λόγῳ ________ ἐλάλησεν.

9. When shall we stand before the king whom we honor?

πότε σταθησόμεθα ἔμπροσθεν τοῦ βασιλέως _______ τιμῶμεν;

10. He taught them by the same parables which we heard.

ἐδίδαξεν αὐτοὺς ἐν ταῖς αὐταῖς παραβολαῖς _________ ἠκούσαμεν.

Exercise 40-C: Supply the correct form of ὅστις so that the Greek sentences will correctly translate the English ones:

1. Where are the men who were speaking in tongues?

ποῦ εἰσιν οἱ ἄνδρες ____________ ἐλάλουν ἐν γλώσσαις;

2. Blessed are the people who received the promises of God.

μακάριος ὁ λαὸς __________ ἔλαβεν τὰς ἐπαγγελίας τοῦ θεοῦ.

3. Jesus sent apostles who prepared the way for him.

ὁ Ἰησοῦς ἔπεμψεν ἀποστόλους ____________ ἡτοίμασαν αὐτῷ τὴν ὁδόν.

4. Lazarus had two sisters who loved Jesus.

εἶχε ὁ Λάζαρος δύο ἀδελφὰς _______ ἠγάπων τὸν Ἰησοῦν.

5. Jesus healed the children who came to him.

ὁ Ἰησοῦς ἐθεράπευσεν τὰ τέκνα ______ ἦλθεν πρὸς αὐτόν.

6. This is the light which lightens every man.

τοῦτό ἐστιν τὸ φῶς _______ φωτίζει πάντας ἀνθρώπους.

7. We have received grace which saves us.

ἐλάβομεν τὴν χάριν _______ ἡμᾶς σῴζει.

8. All those who believe in him will be saved.

πάντες _____________ πιστεύουσιν εἰς αὐτὸν σωθήσονται.

Exercise 40-D: Transform the articular participial expression in each of the following sentences into a relative clause with the same meaning. Be guided by the model provided, noting especially the treatment of the negative:

Model: ὁ μὴ πιστεύων εἰς τὸν υἱὸν οὐκ ἔχει ζωὴν αἰώνιον.

Transform: ὃς οὐ πιστεύει εἰς τὸν υἱὸν οὐκ ἔχει ζωὴν αἰώνιον.

1. ζητοῦσιν τὴν θυγατέρα μου τὴν μὴ ἔχουσαν ἄνδρα. (ὁ ἀνήρ)

___

2. ἔδωκαν ἡμῖν καινὴν ἐντολὴν οἱ ἀκούσαντες τὸν κύριον.

___

3. ἀγαπᾷ ὁ θεὸς τὸν ἄνδρα τὸν ἀγαπῶντα τοὺς ἀδελφούς.

___

4. ἡ ποιοῦσα τὸ θέλημα τοῦ πατρός μου ἀδελφή μού ἐστιν.

___

5. τοῦτό ἐστιν τὸ εὐαγγέλιον τὸ πληροῦν τὸν νόμον. (πληρόω)

___

6. ἀγαπῶμεν τὸν κύριον τὸν διδόντα ἡμῖν τὸν ἄρτον τῆς ζωῆς.

___

7. ἀγαπῶμεν τὸν κύριον τὸν δόντα ἡμῖν τὸν ἄρτον τῆς ζωῆς.

___

8. οὗτός ἐστιν ὁ ποιμὴν ὁ καλός, ὁ τιθεὶς τὴν ψυχὴν αὐτοῦ ὑπὲρ τῶν προβάτων αὐτοῦ.

___

9. δοξάζομεν Ἰησοῦν τὸν θέντα τὴν ψυχὴν αὐτοῦ ὑπὲρ ἡμῶν.

___

10. τιμῶσιν τὸν θεὸν τὸν ἱστάντα τὴν διαθήκην αὐτοῦ τὴν καινὴν πρὸς ἡμᾶς.

____

11. οἱ στάντες πρὸ τοῦ θρόνου εἰσὶν οἱ εἴκοσι τέσσαρες πρεσβύτεροι.

____

12. οἱ μὴ ὄντες μεθ' ἡμῶν καθ' ἡμῶν εἰσιν.

____

13. μακάριοι οἱ σῳζόμενοι.

____

14. ἐδίδασκεν τὰ τέκνα τὰ ἐλθόντα εἰς τὴν πόλιν.

____

15. αἱ θεραπευθεῖσαι ἐθαύμαζον πολύ.

____

<u>Exercise 40-E</u>: Supply the proper relative adjective or adverb (using οἷος, ὅσος, ὅπου, ὅτε, ὅθεν, or ὡς) so that the Greek sentences will correctly render the English ones:

1. He does great wonders, such as we have never seen. ("of such a kind as")
   δυνάμεις μεγάλας ποιεῖ __________ οὐδέποτε εἴδομεν.

2. As many as believe in him will receive power to become sons of God.
   _______ πιστεύουσιν εἰς αὐτὸν δέξονται ἐξουσίαν υἱοὺς θεοῦ γενέσθαι.

3. When I was with them I kept them in your name.
   ______ ἤμην μετ' αὐτῶν, αὐτοὺς ἐτήρουν ἐν τῷ ὀνόματί σου.

4. We were in the house where we saw the Lord.
   ἤμεθα ἐν τῷ οἴκῳ ________ εἴδομεν τὸν κύριον.

5. Then we shall all behold him, when he comes with his angels.

τότε πάντες θεωρήσομεν αὐτόν, ________ ἔρχεται σὺν τοῖς ἀγγέλοις αὐτοῦ.

6. In that day we shall see him as he really is. ("in such a way as")

ἐν τῇ ἡμέρᾳ ἐκείνῃ ὀψόμεθα αὐτὸν ______ ὄντως ἐστίν.

7. He will come quickly, as a bridegroom comes to his bride. ("in such a way as")

ταχέως ἐλεύσεται, _______ νυμφίος πρὸς νύμφην αὐτοῦ ἔρχεται.

8. He went again into the city whence he came with his mother.

πάλιν εἰς τὴν πόλιν ἐπορεύθη ________ ἦλθεν σὺν τῇ μητρὶ αὐτοῦ.

9. I will give you as much as you wish.

δώσω ὑμῖν ____________ βούλεσθε.

10. When Pilate heard this saying, he was more afraid.

_______ ἤκουσεν Πιλᾶτος τοῦτον τὸν λόγον, μᾶλλον ἐφοβήθη.

11. The multitudes were no longer there, where he gave them the loaves.

οἱ ὄχλοι οὐκέτι ἦσαν ἐκεῖ _______ ἔδωκεν αὐτοῖς τοὺς ἄρτους.

12. We have seen such things today as we shall never see again.

σήμερον τοιαῦτα εἴδομεν _________ οὐδέποτε πάλιν ὀψόμεθα.

Exercise 40-F: Supply the relative or interrogative necessary to make the Greek sentences correctly render the English:

1. They asked him where they could buy bread.

αὐτὸν ἠρώτησαν _________ δύνανται ἄρτους ἀγοράσαι.

2. They went into the city where they bought bread.

ἐπορεύθησαν εἰς τὴν πόλιν __________ ἄρτους ἠγόρασαν.

3. Who are causing my people to stumble? (σκανδαλίζω = cause to stumble)

__________ σκανδαλίζουσιν τὸν λαόν μου;

4. I shall lead astray all those who cause my people to stumble.

πλανήσω πάντας __________ τὸν λαόν μου σκανδαλίζουσιν.

5. When we are weak, he will save us.

________ ἀσθενοῦμεν, σώσει ἡμᾶς.

6. We are tempted when we are weak.

πειραζόμεθα ________ ἀσθενοῦμεν.

7. Why does he suffer on our behalf?

________ πάσχει ὑπὲρ ἡμῶν;

8. The high priest asked Pilate whether Jesus would be crucified.

ἠρώτησεν Πιλᾶτον ὁ ἀρχιερεὺς ________ ὁ Ἰησοῦς σταυρωθήσεται.

9. We beheld the place where he healed the blind man.

ἐθεωρήσαμεν τὸν τόπον _______ τὸν τυφλὸν ἐθεράπευσε.

10. No man ever spoke as this man speaks. ("in such a way as")

οὐδεὶς οὐδέποτε ἐλάλησεν ________ λαλεῖ οὗτος.

Exercises to Lesson Forty-One

Exercise 41-A: Given sentences A and B below, together with their translations, translate the remaining Greek sentences into English.

A. οἱ γραμματεῖς ἐζήτησαν τὸν κύριον. The scribes sought the Lord.

B. οἱ Φαρισαῖοι εὗρον τοὺς μαθητάς. The Pharisees found the disciples.

1. οἱ γραμματεῖς καὶ οἱ Φαρισαῖοι ἐζήτησαν τὸν κύριον.

   ____

2. οἱ γραμματεῖς ἐζήτησαν καὶ εὗρον τοὺς μαθητάς.

   ____

3. οἱ γραμματεῖς ἐζήτησαν καὶ τοὺς μαθητάς.

   ____

4. οἱ γραμματεῖς ἐζήτησαν τὸν κύριον, οἱ δὲ Φαρισαῖοι εὗρον τοὺς μαθητάς. ______________________________

   ____

5. οἱ μὲν ἐζήτησαν τὸν κύριον, οἱ δὲ εὗρον τοὺς μαθητάς.

   ____

6. οὔτε οἱ γραμματεῖς οὔτε οἱ Φαρισαῖοι εὗρον τὸν κύριον.

   ____

7. οἱ Φαρισαῖοι ἐζήτησαν καὶ τὸν κύριον καὶ τοὺς μαθητάς.

   ____

8. οὐδὲ οἱ γραμματεῖς ἐζήτησαν τοὺς μαθητάς.

   ____

9. οὐδὲ γὰρ οἱ γραμματεῖς ἐζήτησαν τὸν κύριον, οὐδὲ οἱ Φαρισαῖοι εὗρον τοὺς μαθητάς. ______________________________

   ____

10. οὐ μόνον οἱ γραμματεῖς ἐζήτησαν τὸν κύριον, ἀλλὰ καὶ οἱ Φαρισαῖοι εὗρον τοὺς μαθητάς. ______________________

____

Exercises to Lesson Forty-Two

Exercise 42-A: A number of incomplete statements are given below, and below each of them are a number of words all but one of which will correctly complete the statement. Strike out the word which will not correctly complete the statement above it.

1. English that is frequently a correct translation of Greek

   ὅς ἐκεῖνος ὅτε ὅτι ὅστις

2. English because is frequently a correct translation of Greek

   ὅτι διότι ἐπεί ἐπειδή ὅστις

3. English as is frequently a correct translation of Greek

   ὅτι ὥσπερ καθώς ὡς καθάπερ

4. English and is frequently a correct translation of Greek

   τε δέ ἀλλά καί

5. English but is frequently a correct translation of Greek

   ἀλλά ἄλλα δέ

6. English therefore is frequently a correct translation of Greek

   οὖν ἀλλά ἄρα ὥστε

Exercise 42-B: Same directions as for 42-A.

1. Greek καί is frequently a correct translation of English

   and also too even but both

2. Greek ἤ is frequently a correct translation of English

   or and than either

3. Greek δέ is frequently a correct translation of English

   and but or now yet

4. Greek ὅτι is frequently a correct translation of English

that because when

5. The first word in a clause is never

δέ καί οὖν γάρ τε

Exercise 42-C: Supply the correct word (ὅτι, ὥστε, or the proper case-form of ὅς or ἐκεῖνος so that the Greek will correctly translate the English:

1. We know that man.

γινώσκομεν τὸν ἄνδρα ______________

2. We know that we love God.

γινώσκομεν ________ τὸν θεὸν ἀγαπῶμεν.

3. We know that God loves us.

γινώσκομεν ________ ὁ θεὸς ἡμᾶς ἀγαπᾷ.

4. God loved the world so that he gave his Son.

ἠγάπησεν ὁ θεὸς τὸν κόσμον _________ τὸν υἱὸν αὐτοῦ ἔδωκεν.

5. God loved the world that he made.

ἠγάπησεν ὁ θεὸς τὸν κόσμον ______ ἐποίησεν.

6. God loved the world because he made it.

ἠγάπησεν ὁ θεὸς τὸν κόσμον ________ ἐποίησεν αὐτόν.

7. He healed that blind man.

ἐθεράπευσεν τὸν τυφλὸν ______________

8. He healed the blind man that could not see.

ἐθεράπευσεν τὸν τυφλὸν _______ οὐκ ἐδύνατο βλέπειν.

Exercises to Lesson Forty-Three

Exercise 43-A: Indicate, by placing T or F in the space provided, whether the following statements are true or false:

1. All forms of the aorist imperative have the augment. ( )
2. Some forms of the aorist imperative have the augment. ( )
3. The 2nd pers. pl. pres. indicative active is identical in form to the 2nd pers. pl. pres. imperative active. ( )
4. The 2nd pers. pl. pres. indicative middle and passive is identical in form to the 2nd pers. pl. present imperative middle and passive. ( )
5. The 2nd pers. pl. aorist indicative active is identical in form to the 2nd pers. pl. aorist imperative active. ( )
6. The 2nd pers. pl. aorist indicative middle is identical in form to the 2nd pers. pl. aorist imperative middle. ( )
7. The 2nd pers. pl. aorist indicative passive is identical in form to the 2nd pers. pl. aorist imperative passive. ( )

Exercise 43-B: Refer to Pars. 172 and 326 and form the present imperative active and the present imperative middle and passive of the contract verbs. (The procedure to be followed is indicated for a few forms.)

(a) For αω-verbs:

Present imperative active:

Sg.2. ἀγαπα + # + ε = ἀγάπα

Sg.3. ἀγαπα + ε + τω = ἀγαπάτω

Pl.2. ἀγαπα + ε + τε = ____________

3. ἀγαπα + ε + τωσαν = ____________

Present imperative middle and passive:

Sg.2. ἀγαπα + # + ου = ἀγαπῶ

3. ἀγαπα + ε + σθω = ____________

Pl.2. ἀγαπα + ε + ______ = ____________

3. ______ + ___ + ______ = ____________

(b) For εω-verbs:

Present imperative active:

Sg.2. ποιε + # + ε = ποίει (Contrast 3rd sg. pres. ind. act. ποιεῖ)

3. ποιε + ε + ______ = ____________

Pl.2. ______ + ___ + ______ = ____________

3. ______ + ___ + ______ = ____________

Present imperative middle and passive:

Sg.2. ______ + ___ + ______ = ____________

3. ______ + ___ + ______ = ____________

Pl.2. ______ + ___ + ______ = ____________

3. ______ + ___ + ______ = ____________

(c) For οω-verbs:

Present imperative active:

Sg.2. πληρο + # + ε = πλήρου (Contrast 2nd sg. pres. imp. mid. and pass. πληροῦ)

3. ______ + ___ + ______ = ____________

Pl.2. ______ + ___ + ______ = ____________

3. ______ + ___ + ______ = ____________

Present imperative middle and passive:

Sg.2. ______ + ___ + ______ = πληροῦ

3. ______ + ___ + ______ = ______________

Pl.2. ______ + ___ + ______ = ______________

3. ______ + ___ + ______ = ______________

Exercise 43-C: Fill in the blank spaces in the table below, retaining the person and number of the form given. (Imitate the model.)

(Before attempting this exercise it may be helpful to review Pars. 95 and 126.)

	Present Active Imperative	Present Midd.&Pass. Imperative	Aorist Active Imperative	Aorist Middle Imperative	Aorist Passive Imperative
Model:	λῦε	λύου	λῦσον	λῦσαι	λύθητι
1.	πέμπε				
2.		κρύπτου			
3.			γραφάτω		
4.				κάλυψαι	
5.					βαπτίσθητι
6.	ἀνοιγέτω				
7.		ἐλεγχέσθω			
8.			κηρυξάτω		
9.				διωξάσθωσαν	
10.					ἀχθήτωσαν

<u>Exercise 43-D</u>: Transform the given sentences, which have verbs in the indicative mood, into sentences with verbs in the imperative mood, retaining the person, number, aspect, and voice of the given sentence. Imitate the model.

<u>Model</u>: τὸν νόμον οὐκ ἀκούετε.

<u>Transform</u>: τὸν νόμον μὴ ἀκούετε.

English: Do not hear the law. (= Stop hearing the law.)

1. βλέπει τὸν μαθητήν.

Let him see the disciple.

2. ἔσωσεν τὸν λαὸν αὐτοῦ ἀπὸ τῶν ἁμαρτιῶν αὐτῶν.

Let him save his people from their sins.

3. ἔδωκας αὐτῷ ἐξουσίαν ἐπὶ τῶν ἐθνῶν.

Give him power over the nations.

4. εἰρήνην ἔχουσιν πρὸς τὸν θεόν.

Let them have peace with God.

5. οὐκ ἐσθίουσιν οὐδὲν ἐν ταῖς ἡμέραις ταύταις.

Do not let them eat anything in these days.

6. κατὰ τὴν πίστιν ὑμῶν ἐγενήθη ὑμῖν.

Let it be unto you according to your faith.

7. οὗτοι μεγάλοι ἐκλήθησαν ἐν τοῖς ἔθνεσιν.

Let these men be called great among the gentiles.

8. εἶπες ἡμῖν πότε ταῦτα ἔσται.

Tell us when these things shall be.

9. οὐκ εἶ μαθητὴς ἄπιστος.

Do not be an unfaithful disciple.

10. οὐκ ἔστιν ἁμαρτωλός.

Let him not be a sinner.

11. ἔρχεται μεθ' ἡμῶν.

Let him come with us.

12. ἦλθες μετ' ἐμοῦ.

Come with me.

13. λέγετε ἡμῖν παραβολήν.

Tell us a parable.

14. ἐποιήσατε τὸν δένδρον καλόν.

Make the tree good.

15. ἤκουσε τὴν φωνὴν τοῦ ἀγγέλου.

Let him hear the voice of the angel.

16. δίδως ἡμῖν τὸν ἄρτον τῆς ζωῆς.

Give us the bread of life.

17. ἔλαβεν ποτήριον.

Let him take a cup.

18. πιστεύουσιν εἰς τὸ ὄνομα τοῦ κυρίου.

Let them believe in the name of the Lord.

19. ἔγραψας ἡμῖν καινὴν ἐντολήν.

Write us a new commandment.

20. ἐπορεύθης εἰς τὴν πόλιν τὴν ἁγίαν.

Go into the holy city.

21. σὺ ἔστης ἐκεῖ.

Stand thou there.

22. ἀγαπᾶτε τοὺς ἐχθροὺς ὑμῶν.

Love your enemies.

23. πληροῖς τὴν διακονίαν σου.

Fulfill your ministry.

24. βαπτίζονται ὑπὸ τοῦ προφήτου.

Let them have themselves baptized by the prophet.

25. ἐδέξαντο αὐτὸν ὡς ἀδελφόν.

Let them receive him as a brother.

Exercises to Lesson Forty-Four

Exercise 44-A: In the first column below are listed a number of verb-forms in the indicative mood. Write, in the second column, the corresponding verb-forms of the imperative mood, and, in the third column, the corresponding verb-forms of the subjunctive mood. (Retain the person, number, aspect, and voice of the given form. Refer, if necessary, to Pars. 95 and 126, and be guided by the model given.)

	Indicative	Imperative	Subjunctive
Model:	λύει	λυέτω	λύῃ
1.	κηρύσσεις		
2.	ἀκούουσιν		
3.	ἠκούσατε		
4.	ἑτοιμάζετε		
5.	ἡτοιμάσθη		
6.	εὗρες		
7.	βαπτίζεις		
8.	γράφει		
9.	πέμπετε		
10.	διώκουσιν		
11.	ἐδίωξαν		

	Indicative	Imperative	Subjunctive
12.	δοξάζεται	______	______
13.	ἐβαπτίσατο	______	______
14.	πιστεύεις	______	______
15.	ἐβαπτίσθητε	______	______

Exercise 44-B: Refer to Pars. 172 and 335 and form the present subjunctive active and the present subjunctive middle and passive of the contract verbs. (The procedure to be followed is indicated for a few forms.)

(a) For αω-verbs:

Present subjunctive active:

Sg.1. ἀγαπα + # + ω = ἀγαπῶ
2. ἀγαπα + η + ις = ἀγαπᾷς
3. ἀγαπα + η + ι = ______
Pl.1. ἀγαπα + ___ + ______ = ______
2. ἀγαπα + ___ + ______ = ______
3. ἀγαπα + ___ + ______ = ______

Present subjunctive middle and passive:

Sg.1. ἀγαπα + ___ + ______ = ______
2. ἀγαπα + ___ + ______ = ______
3. ἀγαπα + ___ + ______ = ______
Pl.1. ἀγαπα + ___ + ______ = ______
2. ἀγαπα + ___ + ______ = ______
3. ἀγαπα + ___ + ______ = ______

(b) For εω-verbs:

Present subjunctive active:

Sg.1. ποιε + # + ω = ποιῶ

2. ποιε + η + ις = ποιῇς

3. ποιε + ___ + ________ = ____________________

Pl.1. ποιε + ___ + ________ = ____________________

2. ποιε + ___ + ________ = ____________________

3. ποιε + ___ + ________ = ____________________

Present subjunctive middle and passive:

Sg.1. ποιε + ___ + ________ = ____________________

2. ποιε + ___ + ________ = ____________________

3. ποιε + ___ + ________ = ____________________

Pl.1. ποιε + ___ + ________ = ____________________

2. ποιε + ___ + ________ = ____________________

3. ποιε + ___ + ________ = ____________________

(c) For οω-verbs: (Give the "ideal" contracted forms; some forms which actually are found* are irregular.)

Present subjunctive active: (Note: Combine the stem-formative with the suffix first.)

Sg.1. πληρο + ___ + ________ = ____________________

2. πληρο + ___ + ________ = ____________________

3. πληρο + ___ + ________ = ____________________

Pl.1. πληρο + ___ + ________ = ____________________

2. πληρο + ___ + ________ = ____________________

3. πληρο + ___ + ________ = ____________________

---

* Παραζηλοῦμεν (in 1 Cor 10:22) where we would expect παραζηλῶμεν, and ζηλοῦτε (in Gal 4:17) where we would expect ζηλῶτε, are regarded by most scholars as subjunctives; they are, of course, irregular in form.

Exercise 44-C: Transform the indicative form in each Greek sentence below into a subjunctive form (retain the aspect - present or aorist) so that the transformed sentence will correctly render the English sentence beneath it; change the negatives (οὐ to μή, etc.) if necessary.

Model: οὐκ ἐποιήσατε τὸ δένδρον καλόν.

Transform: μὴ ποιήσητε τὸ δένδρον καλόν.

Don't make the tree good!

1. εἰρήνην ἔχομεν πρὸς τὸν θεόν.

____

Let us have peace with God!

2. ἀγαπῶμεν τοὺς ἐχθροὺς ἡμῶν.

____

Let us love our enemies!

3. οὐκ ἐπορεύθης εἰς τὴν πόλιν τὴν ἁγίαν.

____

Don't go into the holy city!

4. ἐδεξάμεθα αὐτοὺς ὡς ἀδελφούς.

____

Let us receive them as brothers.

5. τί ἐποιήσαμεν;

____

What are we to do?

6. οὐκ ἤλθετε μεθ' ἡμῶν.

____

Don't come with us!

Exercises to Lesson Forty-Five

Exercise 45-A: Transform the relative clauses in the following sentences into indefinite relative clauses (retain the aspect of the verb, but change the mood and introduce ἄν; also change οὐ to μή, etc., if necessary) so that the new Greek sentences will correctly translate the English sentences given:

Model: ὃς ποιεῖ ταῦτα καλῶς ποιεῖ.

Transform: ὃς ἂν ποιῇ ταῦτα καλῶς ποιεῖ.

Whoever does these things does well.

1. ὃς ἀγαπᾷ τὸν ἀδελφὸν αὐτοῦ ἐπλήρωσεν ὅλον τὸν νόμον.

____

Whoever loves his brother has fulfilled the whole law.

2. ὅστις οὐκ ἔδωκεν τὸν ἄρτον τοῖς πτωχοῖς οὐ λήμψεται τὸν ἄρτον τῆς ζωῆς.

____

____

Whoever will not give bread to the poor will not receive the bread of life.

3. ὃς τὴν ψυχὴν αὐτοῦ ὑπὲρ τοῦ εὐαγγελίου ἔθεκεν σωθήσεται ἐν τῇ ἡμέρᾳ τῇ ἐσχάτῃ.

____

____

Whoever lays down his life for the sake of the gospel will be saved in the last day.

4. ὅτε ζητοῦμεν τὸ πρόσωπον αὐτοῦ ἄξει ἡμᾶς εἰς τὴν βασιλείαν αὐτοῦ.

____

Whenever we seek his face he will lead us into his kingdom.

5. ὅσοι γὰρ ἐπίστευσαν εἰς τὸ ὄνομα αὐτοῦ δικαιωθήσονται διὰ τῆς χάριτος αὐτοῦ.

____

____

For as many as (="as many soever") believe in his name will be justified by his grace.

Exercise 45-B: Change the infinitive constructions in the following sentences into clauses introduced by ἵνα. The meaning of the original sentence and that of its transform should be that of the English given.

Model: πιστεύομεν εἰς αὐτὸν εἰς τὸ ἡμῖν δοῦναι αὐτὸν τὸν ἄρτον.
Transform: πιστεύομεν εἰς αὐτὸν ἵνα δῷ ἡμῖν τὸν ἄρτον.

We believe in him in order that he will give us bread.

1. οὐκ εἰμὶ ἐγὼ ἄξιος λῦσαι τὸν ἱμάντα τῶν ὑποδημάτων αὐτοῦ.

____

I am not worthy to loose the thong of his sandals.

2. ἦλθον πληρῶσαι τὸν νόμον.

____

I came to fulfill the law.

3. οἱ ποιμένες ἐζήτουν τὸ παιδίον τοῦ δοξάσαι αὐτό.

____

The shepherds sought the child in order to glorify him.

4. ταῦτα δὲ ἔλεγεν εἰς τὸ πειράσαι αὐτούς.

____

But he said these things to test them.

5. ταῦτα γὰρ ἔγραψα ὑμῖν πρὸς τὸ ὑμᾶς πιστεῦσαι εἰς τὸν κύριον.

____

For I wrote these things to you so that you might believe in the Lord.

Exercise 45-C: Transform the following conditional sentences from Type A to Type B (i.e., so that the transformed sentence correctly renders the English). Caution: It may be necessary to alter the verbs in both clauses.

Model: εἰ ἐποίησεν ταῦτα, καλῶς ἐποίησεν.

Transform: ἐὰν ποιῇ ταῦτα, καλῶς ποιεῖ.

If he does these things, he does well.

1. εἰ οὐκ ἀκούουσιν τὸν νόμον οὐ σωθήσονται.

____

If they do not hear the law, they will not be saved.

2. εἰ οὐκ ἐργάζεται, μὴ ἐσθιέτω.

____

If he does not work, do not let him eat.

3. εἰ ἐλάλεις γλώσσαις, οὐδεὶς ἐνόησεν.

____

If you speak with tongues, no one will understand.

4. εἰ ἐβαπτίσθησαν, σωθήσονται.

____

If they are being baptized, they will be saved.

5. εἰ ἐθεώρεις τὸ πρόσωπον αὐτοῦ, ἐθεράπευέν σε.

____

If you behold his face, he will heal you.

Exercise 45-D: Transform the following conditional sentences from Type B to Type C (i.e., so that the transformed sentence correctly renders the English). Caution: It may be necessary to alter the verbs in both clauses.

Model 1: ἐὰν ποιῇ ταῦτα, καλῶς ποιεῖ.

Transform: εἰ ἐποίει ταῦτα, καλῶς ἂν ἐποίει.

If he were doing these things, he would be doing well.

Model 2: ἐὰν ποιήσῃ ταῦτα, καλῶς ποιήσει.

Transform: εἰ ἐποίησεν ταῦτα, καλῶς ἂν ἐποίησεν.

If he had done these things, he would have done well.

1. ἐὰν ἔλθῃ πρὸς ἡμᾶς, δεξόμεθα αὐτόν.

____

If he had come to us, we would have received him.

2. ἐὰν ποιήσωμεν τὸ θέλημα τοῦ θεοῦ, ἀγαπήσει ἡμᾶς.

____

If we had done the will of God, he would have loved us.

3. ἐὰν ἀγαπήσωμεν αὐτόν, καὶ ἡμᾶς ἀγαπήσει.

____

If we had loved him, he would have also loved us.

4. ἐὰν μηδεὶς κηρύξῃ τὸν λόγον τῆς ἀληθείας, οὐκ αὐτὸν ἀκούσουσιν.

____

If no one had preached the word of truth, they would not have heard it.

5. ἐὰν τηρήσωμεν τὰς ἐντολὰς αὐτοῦ, ἐσόμεθα ὡς τέκνα θεοῦ.

____

If we were keeping his commandments, we would be as children of God.

Exercises to Lesson Forty-Six

Exercise 46-A: Write out the required principal parts of the compound verbs listed below, modelling them on the principal parts given for the simple verbs:

	Present	Future	Aorist	Aorist Passive
1.	λύω, loose, set free	λύσω	ἔλυσα	ἐλύθην
	ἀπολύω, dismiss	________	________	________
2.	ἄρχω, rule	ἄρξω	ἦρξα	ἤρχθην
	ὑπάρχω, be, exist	________	________	(None)
3.	ἄγω, lead	ἄξω	ἤγαγον	ἤχθην
	συνάγω, gather	________	________	________
	ὑπάγω, go	________	________	(None)
4.	ἐρωτάω, ask	ἐρωτήσω	ἠρώτησα	ἠρωτήθην
	ἐπερωτάω, ask	________	________	________
5.	καλέω, call	καλέσω	ἐκάλεσα	ἐκλήθην
	παρακαλέω, beseech, comfort	________	________	________
6.	πατέω, tread	πατήσω	ἐπάτησα	ἐπατήθην
	περιπατέω, walk, go; behave, live	________	________	(None)
7.	-κυνέω	-κυνήσω	-εκύνησα	(None)
	προσκυνέω, worship	________	________	(None)
8.	βάλλω, throw, put	βαλῶ	ἔβαλον	ἐβλήθην
	ἐκβάλλω, cast out	________	________	________
9.	-στέλλω	-στελῶ	-έστειλα	-εστάλην
	ἀποστέλλω, send	________	________	________

	Present		Future	Aorist	Aorist Passive
10.	-κτείνω		-κτενῶ	-έκτεινα	-εκτάνθην
	ἀποκτείνω,	kill	________	________	________
11.	ἔρχομαι,	come, go	ἐλεύσομαι	ἦλθον	(None)
	ἀπέρχομαι,	depart	________	________	(None)
	ἐξέρχομαι,	go out	________	________	(None)
	εἰσέρχομαι,	enter	________	________	(None)
	προσέρχομαι,	approach	________	________	(None)
12.	εὔχομαι,	pray	εὔξομαι	εὐξάμην	(None)
	προσεύχομαι,	pray	________	________	(None)
13.	κρίνομαι, (Mid.&Pass. < κρίνω, judge)	be judged	κρινοῦμαι	ἐκρινάμην	ἐκρίθην
	ἀποκρίνομαι,	answer	________	________	________
14.	-βαίνω		-βήσομαι	-έβην	(None)
	ἀναβαίνω,	go up	________	________	(None)
	καταβαίνω,	go down	________	________	(None)
15.	-θνήσκω		-θανοῦμαι	-έθανον	(None)
	ἀποθνήσκω,	die	________	________	(None)
16.	-ἵημι		-ἥσω	-ἧκα	-ἕθην
	ἀφίημι,	permit; forgive	________	________	________
17.	δίδωμι,	give	δώσω	ἔδωκα	ἐδόθην
	ἀποδίδωμι,	give away, give back, render	________	________	________
	παραδίδωμι,	betray, hand over, hand on	________	________	________
18.	γινώσκω,	know	γνώσομαι	ἔγνων	ἐγνώσθην
	ἐπιγινώσκω,	know, understand, recognize	________	________	________

<u>Exercise 46-B</u>: Put an X in each of the appropriate spaces; if a form may be either middle <u>or</u> passive, put an X in <u>both</u> spaces. Imitate the model:

	Person			Number		Pres.	Impf.	Aor.	Fut.	Act.	Mid.	Pass.	Indic.	Subj.	Imper.
	1	2	3	Sg	Pl										
Model: ἀπελύετο			X	X			X				X	X	X		
1. συναχθῶσιν															
2. παρεκλήθητε															
3. παρακλήθητε															
4. παρακληθῆτε															
5. παρακλήθητι															
6. ἐξέβαλλε															
7. ἐξέβαλε															
8. ἔκβαλλε															
9. ἀποκτείνομεν															
10. ἀποκτενοῦμεν															
11. ἀποκτανθήτω															
12. ἀπεκτείνομεν															
13. ἀπεκτείναμεν															
14. ἀποστελῶ															
15. ἀποστείλω															
16. ἀποσταλῶ															
17. περιπατοῦμεν															
18. περιπατῶμεν															
19. περιεπατοῦμεν															
20. προσκυνήσωσιν															

Exercise 46-C: Transform the sentences below into sentences of equivalent meaning, but with verbs in the passive voice. Imitate the model given:

Model: ὁ πατὴρ ἀπέστειλεν τὸν υἱὸν αὐτοῦ εἰς τὸν κόσμον.

Transform: ὁ υἱὸς αὐτοῦ ἀπεστάλη εἰς τὸν κόσμον ὑπὸ τοῦ πατρός.

1. οἱ στρατιῶται τὸν διδάσκαλον τὸν δίκαιον ἀπέκτειναν.

____

2. παρέδωκεν ὁ Ἰούδας τὸν υἱὸν τοῦ ἀνθρώπου.

____

3. παρακαλέσει ὁ κύριος τὰς καρδίας τῶν ἁγίων.

____

4. ὁ μαθητὴς ἐξέβαλεν πολλὰ δαιμόνια.

____

5. οἱ ἀπόστολοι συνήγαγον τὴν ἐκκλησίαν.

____

6. ἀπέλυσεν ὁ Πιλᾶτος τὸν Βαραββᾶν.

____

7. οἱ Φαρισαῖοι ἐπηρώτησαν τὸν Ἰησοῦν περὶ τῶν σημείων.

____

8. παραδώσουσιν οἱ ἀπόστολοι τὸ εὐαγγέλιον.

____

9. ὁ κύριος ἀποστελεῖ τὸν ἄγγελον πρὸς τὸν λαόν.

____

10. παρακαλοῦμεν ὑμᾶς.

____

Exercise 46-D: In each group of sentences below, supply the proper form of the required verb, so that the Greek will correctly render the English given above it:

1. Supply the proper form of ἀπολύω:

(a) Jesus dismisses the multitudes.
ὁ Ἰησοῦς ______________ τοὺς ὄχλους.

(b) Pilate released Barabbas to them. (Aorist)
ὁ Πιλᾶτος ______________ αὐτοῖς τὸν Βαραββᾶν.

(c) When he had dismissed the multitude, he went up into the mountain.
______________ τὸν ὄχλον, ἀνέβη εἰς τὸ ὄρος.

(d) Pilate wanted to release Jesus.
ὁ Πιλᾶτος ἤθελεν τὸν Ἰησοῦν ______________

(e) They were dismissed with peace from the brethren. (Aorist)
______________ μετ' εἰρήνης ἀπὸ τῶν ἀδελφῶν.

2. Supply the proper form of ἀναβαίνω:

(a) Who will ascend into heaven?
τίς ______________ εἰς τὸν οὐρανόν;

(b) He is also the one who ascended.
αὐτός ἐστιν καὶ ὁ ______________

(c) The disciples went up into the city. (Aorist)
______________ οἱ μαθηταὶ εἰς τὴν πόλιν.

(d) We are going up to Jerusalem.
______________ εἰς Ἱεροσόλυμα.

(e) We are about to go up to Jerusalem. (Present infinitive)
μέλλομεν ______________ εἰς Ἱεροσόλυμα.

3. Supply the proper form of καταβαίνω:

(a) Let him come down now from the cross. (Aorist)

_______________ νῦν ἀπὸ τοῦ σταυροῦ.

(b) I am the bread which came down from heaven.

ἐγώ εἰμι ὁ ἄρτος ὁ ἐκ τοῦ οὐρανοῦ _______________

(c) The Lord himself will descend from heaven.

αὐτὸς ὁ κύριος _______________ ἀπ' οὐρανοῦ.

(d) I saw the holy city, New Jerusalem, coming down out of heaven from God.

τὴν πόλιν τὴν ἁγίαν 'Ιερουσαλὴμ καινὴν εἶδον _______________ ἐκ τοῦ οὐρανοῦ ἀπὸ τοῦ θεοῦ.

4. Supply the proper form of γινώσκω:

(a) The world did not know him. (Aorist)

ὁ κόσμος αὐτὸν οὐκ _______________

(b) You will know the truth.

_______________ τὴν ἀλήθειαν.

(c) I never knew you. (Aorist)

οὐδέποτε _______________ ὑμᾶς.

(d) How will that which is spoken be known?

πῶς _______________ τὸ λαλούμενον;

(e) I came in order that you may know the truth.

ἦλθον ἵνα _______________ τὴν ἀλήθειαν.

(f) He sent his son, who did not know sin. (Aorist)

ἀπέστειλεν τὸν υἱὸν αὐτοῦ τὸν μὴ _______________ ἁμαρτίαν.

(g) Do not let your left hand know what your right hand is doing. (Aorist)

μὴ _______________ ἡ ἀριστερά σου τί ποιεῖ ἡ δεξιά σου.

5. Supply the proper form of ἀνίστημι:

(Note: ἀνίστημι is transitive in the future and 1st aorist active, and means raise, erect, raise up; it is intransitive in the 2nd aorist and in all middle forms, and then means rise, stand up, get up.)

(a) I will raise him up at the last day.

_______________ αὐτὸν ἐν τῇ ἐσχάτῃ ἡμέρᾳ.

(b) God raised him from the dead.

ὁ θεὸς _______________ αὐτὸν ἐκ νεκρῶν.

(c) After he raised him from the dead God exalted him even unto heaven.

_______________ αὐτὸν ἐκ νεκρῶν ὁ θεὸς ὕψωσεν αὐτὸν καὶ ἕως οὐρανοῦ.

(d) He will rise on the third day.

τῇ τρίτῃ ἡμέρᾳ _______________

(e) Having risen, he went to his father.

_______________ ἦλθεν πρὸς τὸν πατέρα αὐτοῦ.

(f) They rose up to play.

_______________ παίζειν.

6. Supply the proper form of ἐγείρω: (Active, raise; passive, rise, be raised)

(a) God raised him from the dead.

ὁ θεὸς _______________ αὐτὸν ἐκ νεκρῶν.

(b) Christ rose from the dead.

_______________ ὁ Χριστὸς ἐκ νεκρῶν.

(c) For nation shall rise against nation.

_______________ γὰρ ἔθνος ἐπ' ἔθνος.

(d) He who raised Christ Jesus from the dead will raise us also on the last day.

ὁ _______________ ἐκ νεκρῶν Χριστὸν 'Ιησοῦν _______________ καὶ ἡμᾶς ἐν τῇ ἐσχάτῃ ἡμέρᾳ.

7. Supply the proper form of ἀποκρίνομαι, answer (+ dat. of person) or ἐπερωτάω, ask (someone something: two accusatives):

(a) If you ask me these things I will answer you.

ἐὰν ________________ με ταῦτα ________________ σοι.

(b) If you were asking me these things I would answer you.

εἰ ________________ με ταῦτα ________________ ἄν σοι.

(c) If you had asked me these things I would have answered you.

εἰ ________________ με ταῦτα ________________ ἄν σοι.

(d) No one could answer those who were asking these things.

οὐκ ἠδύνατο οὐδεὶς ________________ τοῖς ________________ ταῦτα.

8. Supply the proper form of μένω:

(a) He who abides in me does the works.

ὁ ἐν ἐμοὶ ____________ ποιεῖ τὰ ἔργα.

(b) If you do not abide in the vine you will not be my disciples.

ἐὰν μὴ ______________ ἐν τῇ ἀμπέλῳ οὐκ ἔσεσθε μαθηταί μου.

(c) He went in to stay with them.

εἰσῆλθεν τοῦ ____________ σὺν αὐτοῖς.

(d) Let brotherly love continue (= keep on remaining).

ἡ φιλαδελφία ________________

9. Supply the proper form of κεῖμαι:

(a) And already the ax lies at the root of the trees.

ἤδη δὲ ἡ ἀξίνη πρὸς τὴν ῥίζαν τῶν δένδρων ____________

(b) Come, see the place where he was lying.

δεῦτε ἴδετε τὸν τόπον ὅπου ________________

(c) You will find a babe, lying in a manger. (βρέφος is neuter)

εὑρήσετε βρέφος ________________ ἐν φάτνῃ.

10. Supply the proper form of λέγω:

(Note: In the aorist passive λέγω uses the forms ἐρρέθην and ἐρρήθην; the former is more common in the indicative, but the aorist passive participle is usually formed from the latter; when the augment of this form is removed, the first ρ is removed as well (and, conventionally, a rough breathing is placed over the remaining ρ: ῥηθείς).

(a) Jesus began to speak to the crowds about John.

ἤρξατο ὁ Ἰησοῦς ____________ τοῖς ὄχλοις περὶ Ἰωάννου.

(b) But he said to her, "What do you want?"

ὁ δὲ ____________ αὐτῇ, τί θέλεις;

(c) That which was spoken by the prophet was fulfilled.

ἐπληρώθη τὸ ____________ διὰ τοῦ προφήτου.

(d) I will tell you by what authority I do these things.

ἐγὼ ὑμῖν ____________ ἐν ποίᾳ ἐξουσίᾳ ταῦτα ποιῶ.

(e) The promises were spoken to Abraham.

τῷ δὲ Ἀβραὰμ ______________ αἱ ἐπαγγελίαι.

11. Supply the proper form of κάθημαι:

(a) The people who were sitting in darkness have seen a great light.

ὁ λαὸς ὁ ________________ ἐν σκοτίᾳ φῶς εἶδεν μέγα.

(b) Jesus sat beside the sea.

ὁ Ἰησοῦς _______________ παρὰ τὴν θάλασσαν.

(c) You shall sit upon twelve thrones.

__________________ ὑμεῖς ἐπὶ δώδεκα θρόνους.

(d) Sit (sg.) there under my footstool.

_______________ ἐκεῖ ὑπὸ τὸν ὑποπόδιόν μου.

12. Supply the proper form of ἀφίημι, leave, forgive (in the latter meaning with dative of the person forgiven and accusative of the thing forgiven):

(a) The fever left her.

_____________ αὐτὴν ὁ πυρετός.

(b) Your heavenly Father will forgive you also.

_________________ καὶ ὑμῖν ὁ πατὴρ ὑμῶν ὁ οὐράνιος.

(c) Forgive us our debts as we also forgive our debtors.

_________ ἡμῖν τὰ ὀφειλήματα ἡμῶν, ὡς καὶ ἡμεῖς ____________ τοῖς ὀφειλέταις ἡμῶν.

(d) Your sins are forgiven. (Present passive)

_____________________ σου αἱ ἁμαρτίαι.

(e) The Son of man has power to forgive sins on earth.

ἐξουσίαν ἔχει ὁ υἱὸς τοῦ ἀνθρώπου _________________ ἁμαρτίας ἐπὶ τῆς γῆς.

13. Supply the proper form of ἀπόλλυμι:

(a) Have you come to destroy us? (Aorist)

ἦλθες _______________ ἡμᾶς;

(b) For whoever wishes to save his life will lose it, and whoever loses his life for my sake, (the latter) will save it.

ὃς γὰρ ἂν θέλῃ τὴν ψυχὴν αὐτοῦ σῶσαι _________________ αὐτήν, ὃς δ'ἂν _______________ (Aorist) τὴν ψυχὴν αὐτοῦ ἕνεκεν ἐμοῦ οὗτος σώσει αὐτὴν.

(c) For as many as sinned without the law will also perish without law.

ὅσοι γὰρ ἀνόμως ἥμαρτον ἀνόμως καὶ _____________________

(d) They were destroyed by serpents. (Imperfect)

ὑπὸ τῶν ὄφεων _____________________

14. Supply the proper form of ζάω:

(a) I am the living bread.

ἐγώ εἰμι ὁ ἄρτος ὁ ________

(b) Why do you seek the living among the dead?

τί ζητεῖτε τὸν __________ μετὰ τῶν νεκρῶν;

(c) Your son lives.

ὁ υἱός σου ________

(d) The righteous shall live by faith.

ὁ δὲ δίκαιος ἐκ πίστεως __________

(e) Once I was alive apart from law.

ἐγὼ δὲ __________ χωρὶς νόμου ποτέ.

15. Supply the proper form of δείκνυμι:

(a) Show (sg.) me your faith apart from works, and I by my works will show you my faith.

__________ μοι τὴν πίστιν σου χωρὶς τῶν ἔργων, κἀγώ σοι

__________ ἐκ τῶν ἔργων μου τὴν πίστιν.

(b) He shows him all the kingdoms of the world.

__________ αὐτῷ πάσας τὰς βασιλείας τοῦ κόσμου.

(c) He showed me the holy city.

__________ μοι τὴν πόλιν τὴν ἁγίαν.

(d) God sent his angel to show these things to his servants. (Aorist)

ὁ θεὸς ἀπέστειλεν τὸν ἄγγελον αὐτοῦ __________

ταῦτα τοῖς δούλοις αὐτοῦ.

Exercises to Lesson Forty-Seven

Exercise 47-A: Give the first person singular indicative of (1) the perfect active, and (2) the perfect middle and passive of each of the following verbs:

	Perfect Active	Perfect Middle & Passive
1. κοπιάω, work	__________	__________
2. ἀπατάω, deceive	__________	__________
3. φορέω, wear	__________	__________
4. σκοπέω, notice	__________	__________
5. θαυμάζω, marvel	__________	__________
6. πωρόω, harden	__________	__________
7. σταυρόω, crucify	__________	__________
8. ζημιόω, injure	__________	__________

Exercise 47-B: Identify the tense of each of the following forms of the verb ἁγιάζω, sanctify, consecrate, by putting an X in the appropriate space below:

	Present	Imperf.	Future	Aorist	Perfect	Pluperfect
1. ἁγιάσετε						
2. ἡγιάσατε						
3. ἡγιάκατε						
4. ἡγιάσμην						
5. ἡγιασάμην						
6. ἡγίασμαι						

(Exercise 47-B, Cont.)

	Present	Imperf.	Future	Aorist	Perfect	Pluperfect
7. ἁγιάσει						
8. ἡγιάκει						
9. ἡγιάζετε						
10. ἁγιάζετε						

Exercise 47-C: Transform the sentences below into sentences with passive verbs, but otherwise equivalent in meaning; retain the perfect tense in each case, but adjust the person and number of the verb if necessary. Imitate the model given:

Model: ὁ προφήτης τὸν μαθητὴν βεβάπτικεν.

Transform: ὁ μαθητὴς ὑπὸ τοῦ προφήτου βεβάπτισται.

1. ὁ πατὴρ τὸν υἱὸν ἀπέσταλκεν.

2. ὁ κύριος αὐτὸς τὸν νόμον πεπλήρωκε.

3. καὶ τοὺς τυφλοὺς καὶ τοὺς κωφοὺς τεθεράπευκας.

4. τὴν θύραν ὑπὲρ ἡμῶν ἀνεῴγατε.

5. ἡτοίμακεν ὁ Ἰωάννης τὴν ὁδὸν ἐν τῇ ἐρήμῳ.

6. ὁ Χριστὸς ἡμῖν δέδωκεν ζωὴν αἰώνιον. (Make ζωὴν αἰώνιον the subject)

7. ταῦτα πάντα εἰς βιβλίον γέγραφεν ὁ προφήτης.

8. οἱ πονηροὶ ἐσταυρώκασιν τὸν υἱὸν τοῦ ἀνθρώπου.

9. ἐν ἀρχῇ ἔγνωκάς με.

10. οὐκ εἰλήφατε τὸν κύριον.

____

<u>Exercise 47-D</u>: On the lines marked (a) below, rewrite the sentences of Exercise 47-C, but change the verbs to pluperfect active; then, on the lines marked (b), write the passive transform of each of these (use the augment where possible, as in the model):

<u>Model</u>: (a) ὁ προφήτης τὸν μαθητὴν ἐβεβαπτίκει.

<u>Transform</u>: (b) ὁ μαθητὴς ὑπὸ τοῦ προφήτου ἐβεβάπτιστο.

1. (a) ______________________________

   (b) ______________________________

2. (a) ______________________________

   (b) ______________________________

3. (a) ______________________________

   (b) ______________________________

4. (a) ______________________________

   (b) ______________________________

5. (a) ______________________________

   (b) ______________________________

6. (a) ______________________________

   (b) ______________________________

7. (a) ______________________________

   (b) ______________________________

8. (a) ______________________________

   (b) ______________________________

9. (a) ______________________________

   (b) ______________________________

10. (a) ______________________________

    (b) ______________________________

Exercise 47-E: A number of pairs of sentences are given below. Combine the two into one which will translate the English sentence given, as illustrated in the model:

Model: πεφανέρωται ἡμῖν. σώσει ἡμᾶς.

Combination: ὁ πεφανερωμένος ἡμῖν σώσει ἡμᾶς.

He who has been revealed to us will save us.

1. δοξάσωμεν τὸν κύριον. τεθεράπευκεν τοὺς ἀσθενοῦντας.

Let us glorify the Lord who has healed the sick.

2. δὸς ἡμῖν τὸν ἄρτον ἡμῶν. ἀφήκαμεν τοῖς ὀφειλέταις ἡμῶν.

Give bread to us who have forgiven our debtors.

3. ὁ Χριστὸς ἐγήγερται ἐκ νεκρῶν. οἱ μαθηταὶ ἐχάρησαν.

After Christ had risen (=been raised) from the dead, the disciples rejoiced.

4. βεβαπτίσμεθα. δικαιωθησόμεθα.

Since we have been baptized, we shall be justified.

5. εὑρήκασιν τὸν Χριστόν. οὐκέτι ζητήσουσιν αὐτόν.

When they have found the Messiah they will no longer seek him.

6. οὐκ οἴδασιν τὰς γραφάς. οὐ πιστεύουσιν εἰς αὐτόν.

Because they do not know the scriptures they do not believe in him.

7. ἕστηκα ἐπὶ τὴν θύραν. κρούει ὁ κύριος.

The Lord who stands at the door is knocking.

Exercises to Lesson Forty-Eight

Exercise 48-A: Change the genitives of the reflexives in the sentences below to forms of ἴδιος, so that the meaning in each sentence is unchanged:

1. ἦλθεν εἰς τὴν ἑαυτοῦ πόλιν.

   ____

2. ἑκάστη τὸν ἑαυτῆς ἄνδρα ἐχέτω.

   ____

3. ἐνέδυσεν αὐτὸν τὰ ἱμάτια ἑαυτοῦ.

   ____

4. ἕκαστος δὲ τὸν ἑαυτοῦ μισθὸν λήμψεται.

   ____

5. δέξονταί με εἰς τοὺς οἴκους ἑαυτῶν.

   ____

Exercise 48-B: Complete the Greek sentences so that they will correctly render the corresponding English ones. Use forms of the reflexive pronouns, only:

1. I shall draw all men to myself.
   πάντας ἑλκύσω πρὸς ______________

2. I can do nothing of myself.
   οὐ δύναμαι ἐγὼ ποιεῖν ἀπ' ________________ οὐδέν.

3. You do not have the love of God in yourselves.
   τὴν ἀγάπην τοῦ θεοῦ οὐκ ἔχετε ἐν ________________

4. Let us cleanse ourselves from every defilement of the flesh.
καθαρίσωμεν ________________ ἀπὸ παντὸς μολυσμοῦ σαρκός.

5. For we preach not ourselves.
οὐ γὰρ κηρύσσομεν ________________

6. He made himself Son of God.
υἱὸν θεοῦ ____________ ἐποίησεν.

7. Then the Jews said to each other, . . .
εἶπον οὖν οἱ Ἰουδαῖοι πρὸς ________________

8. The sisters said to each other, . . .
αἱ ἀδελφαὶ ἔλεγον πρὸς ______________

9. They trimmed their lamps (i.e., their own lamps).
ἐκόσμησαν τὰς λαμπάδας _______________

10. Every kingdom divided against itself is laid waste.
πᾶσα βασιλεία μερισθεῖσα καθ' ____________ ἐρημοῦται.

Exercise 48-C: Complete the Greek sentences so that they will correctly render the corresponding English ones. Use forms of the reciprocal pronoun, only:

1. Pray for each other.
προσεύχεσθε ὑπὲρ _______________

2. Let us love one another.
ἀγαπῶμεν ______________

3. Therefore confess (your) sins to one another.
ἐξομολογεῖσθε οὖν _______________ τὰς ἁμαρτίας.

4. The sisters gave gifts to each other.
αἱ ἀδελφαὶ δῶρα ἔδωκαν _______________

5. Bear each other's burdens.

_______________ τὰ βάρη βαστάζετε.

Exercise 48-D: Supply the correct form of τις, τι in the blank spaces in the Greek sentences so that they will correctly translate the English sentences:

1. Someone gave them the loaves.
   ἔδωκέν _______ τοὺς ἄρτους αὐτοῖς.

2. He gave someone the loaves.
   ἔδωκέν _______ τοὺς ἄρτους.

3. He gave them something.
   ἔδωκέν ______ αὐτοῖς.

4. Some of the disciples are seeking the Lord.
   ζητοῦσιν τὸν κύριόν ________ τῶν μαθητῶν.

5. The Lord will be found by somebody.
   εὑρηθήσεται ὁ κύριος ὑπό ____________

6. The Lord will be found by certain ones.
   εὑρηθήσεται ὁ κύριος ὑπό ____________

7. The Lord will be found by some of the disciples.
   ὁ κύριος εὑρηθήσεται ὑπό ___________ ἐκ τῶν μαθητῶν.

8. The Lord found some of the disciples.
   ὁ κύριος εὗρέν _________ τῶν μαθητῶν.

9. The Lord found somebody.
   ὁ κύριος εὗρέν __________

10. The Lord found something.
    ὁ κύριος εὗρέν ________

11. The Lord gave the loaves to some of the disciples.
    ἔδωκεν ὁ κύριος τοὺς ἄρτους__________ τῶν μαθητῶν.

12. He did some works.
    ἔργα ________ ἐποίησεν.

Exercise 48-E: Supply ποτε, που, μή ποτε, μή που, μή πως, or εἴ πως so that the Greek sentences will correctly translate the English:

1. For you were once darkness, but now you are light in the Lord.
   ἦτε γάρ _______ σκότος νῦν δὲ φῶς ἐν κυρίῳ.

2. I fear lest somehow I may be preaching the gospel in vain.
   φοβοῦμαι _______________ εἰκῇ εὐαγγελίσωμαι.

3. We shall find them somewhere.
   εὑρήσομέν __________ αὐτούς.

4. We besought the Lord whether he had perhaps hardened the hearts of his people.
   ἐδεήθημεν τῷ κυρίῳ ____________ ἐπώρωσεν τὰς καρδίας τοῦ λαοῦ αὐτοῦ.

5. Let us be watchful, so that the Lord will not find us sleeping.
   γρηγορῶμεν ______________ ἡμᾶς εὕρῃ ὁ κύριος καθεύδοντας.

6. They were formerly hated, but now they are beloved.
   ἐμισήθησάν ____________ νῦν δὲ ἀγαπῶνται.

7. The prophet says these things somewhere.
   ταῦτά φησι ____________ ὁ προφήτης.

8. Let us flee, lest our enemies seize us.
   φεύγωμεν ______________ πιάσωσιν ἡμᾶς οἱ ἐχθροὶ ἡμῶν.

9. Once we were few, but now we are many.
   ἤμεθα μέν ____________ ὀλίγοι, νῦν δὲ πολλοί.

10. At some time we shall see each other again.
    πάλιν ὀψόμεθά ______________ ἀλλήλους.

Exercises to Lesson Forty-Nine

__Exercise 49-A__: In each group of sentences below, sentence (b) is the translation of sentence (a); using these as guides, translate sentence (c) into Greek, using the vocative wherever possible (remembering to omit the article):

1. (a) Therefore the man is without excuse.
   (b) διὸ ἀναπολόγητος ὁ ἄνθρωπος.
   (c) Therefore you are without excuse, O man.

____

2. (a) Where is the victory of death? Where is the sting of Hell?
   (b) ποῦ τὸ νῖκος τοῦ θανάτου; ποῦ τὸ κέντρον τοῦ ᾅδου;
   (c) O death, where is thy victory? O Hell, where is thy sting?

____

3. (a) The Lord taught us to pray.
   (b) ὁ κύριος ἐδίδαξεν ἡμᾶς προσεύχεσθαι.
   (c) Lord, teach us to pray.

____

4. (a) I shall follow my teacher.
   (b) τῷ διδασκάλῳ μου ἀκολουθήσω.
   (c) O teacher, I shall follow thee.

____

(a) The Father heard our prayers.
(b) ὁ πατὴρ ἤκουσεν τῶν προσευχῶν ἡμῶν.
(c) Father, hear our prayers.

____

6. (a) His daughter has been healed.

   (b) ἡ θυγάτηρ αὐτοῦ ἐθεραπεύθη.

   (c) O daughter, be healed.

   ____

7. (a) The woman touched his garment.

   (b) ἡ γυνὴ ἥψατο τοῦ ἱματίου αὐτοῦ.

   (c) O woman, touch his garment.

   ____

8. (a) The man went away.

   (b) ὁ ἀνὴρ ἀπῆλθεν.

   (c) O man, go away.

   ____

9. (a) We do not fear the king.

   (b) οὐ φοβούμεθα τὸν βασιλέα.

   (c) O king, we do not fear thee.

   ____

10. (a) The vain hypocrite will perish.

   (b) ὁ κενὸς ὑποκριτὴς ἀπολεῖται.

   (c) Vain hypocrite, you will perish.

   ____

Exercise 49-B: Supply the missing Greek forms. (In this exercise, use the genitive with the verbs in Par. 382(3), and the dative with those in Par. 382(4).) A few words of necessary vocabulary are supplied.

1. ἐκκλησία, ας, ἡ, <u>church</u>

(a) The bishop rules the church.

ὁ ἐπίσκοπος ἄρχει ____________________

(b) The sinner does not obey the church.

ὁ ἁμαρτωλὸς οὐχ ὑπακούει ________________

(c) The bishops rule the churches.

οἱ ἐπίσκοποι ἄρχουσιν ____________________

(d) The sinners will obey the churches.

οἱ ἁμαρτωλοὶ ὑπακούσουσιν ________________

2. βασιλεία, ας, ἡ, <u>kingdom</u>, <u>kingship</u>

(a) We long for the kingdom of God.

ἐπιθυμοῦμεν ____________________ τοῦ θεοῦ.

(b) The apostle drew near to the kingdom.

ἤγγισεν ὁ ἀπόστολος ____________________

(c) They do not desire the kingdom.

οὐκ____

(d) The sinners do not approach the kingdom.

____

3. ἄγγελος, ου, ὁ, <u>angel</u>

(a) She disbelieved the angel.

ἠπίστει ____________________

(b) We cannot touch angels.

οὐ δυνάμεθα ἅπτεσθαι ____________________

(c) We do not disbelieve angels.

οὐκ__________________________________

(d) He is not touching the angel.

οὐχ ______________________________

4. ἀρχιερεύς, έως, ὁ, chief priest

(a) Let him follow the chief priest.

ἀκολουθείτω ______________________

(b) Let him hear the chief priest.

ἀκουέτω ______________________

(c) We were following the chief priests.

____

(d) We have heard the chief priests.

____

5. δύναμις, εως, ἡ, power, strength, ability; mighty work, miracle

(a) The weak lack strength.

οἱ ἀσθενεῖς ὑστεροῦσιν ______________________

(b) The ruler did not use his power.

ὁ ἄρχων οὐκ ἐχρήσατο ______________________

(c) The weak man lacked strength.

____

6. ἀνήρ, ἀνδρός, ὁ, man

(a) We remember this man.

μνημονεύομεν ______________________

(b) You serve that man.

δουλεύετε ______________________

(c) I shall remember that man.

____

(d) They will serve these men.

____

7. προφήτης, ου, ὁ, prophet; πνεῦμα, -ματος, τό, spirit

(a) God fills his prophets with his spirit.

πληροῖ ὁ θεὸς ______________________________________

(b) The prophets have been filled with the spirit.

____

(c) God entrusted the prophets with the spirit. (See Par. 382(4)(a), fn.2.)

____

8. χάρις, χάριτος, ἡ, grace; ἀπόστολος, ου, ὁ, apostle

(a) God has filled his apostle with his grace.

ἔπλησεν ὁ θεὸς ______________________________________

(b) The apostle is filled with God's grace.

ἐπλήσθη ______________________________________

(c) The apostle thanks God for his grace. (See Par. 382(4)(a),fn.1.)

____

Exercise 49-C: Supply the missing Greek forms. (In this exercise, use the genitive or dative with the adjectives involved, as indicated in the Lesson.) A few words of necessary vocabulary are supplied.

1. οἶνος, ου, ὁ, wine

(a) He took a cup full of wine.

ἔλαβεν ποτήριον μεστὸν ________________

(b) They took cups full of wine.

ἔλαβον ποτήρια ____________________

2. γονεύς, έως, ὁ, <u>parent</u>

(a) The child is disobedient to his parents.
τὸ τέκνον ἐστὶν ἀπειθὲς ________________ αὐτοῦ.

(b) The children were disobedient to their parents.

____

3. μισθός, οῦ, ὁ, <u>wages</u>, <u>reward</u>

(a) The workman is worthy of his wages. (Use Sg. of "wages")
ἄξιος ὁ ἐργάτης ________________ αὐτοῦ.

(b) The workmen are worthy of their wages. (Use Pl. of "wages")

____

4. λαός, οῦ, ὁ, <u>people</u>

(a) I have done nothing hostile to the people.
ἐγὼ οὐδὲν ἐποίησα ἐναντίον ________________

(b) The winds were contrary to them.
οἱ ἄνεμοι ἦσαν ________________

5. κλάσμα, -ματος, τό, <u>fragment</u>

(a) They took up twelve baskets full of fragments.
ἦραν δώδεκα κοφίνους πλήρεις ________________

(b) We took up one basket full of fragments.

____

Exercises to Lesson Fifty

Exercise 50-A: In the left-hand column below a number of verb-forms are given in the indicative mood. Supply, in the other columns, the corresponding forms of the subjunctive, imperative, and optative moods; in each case retain the person, number, tense, and voice of the given indicative form. Imitate the model:

Indicative	Subjunctive	Imperative	Optative
Model: λύει	λύῃ	λυέτω	λύοι
1. γράφεις			
2. ἐστίν			
3. ἐλάβετε			
4. γινώσκεις			
5. ἔρχεται			
6. ἦλθες			
7. ἐπλήρωσαν			
8. ἐβαπτίσθης			
9. ἐδίωξας			
10. ἐθεάσω (from θεάομαι)			

Exercise 50-B: Given the direct questions below, rewrite them as indirect, first using the indicative, then the optative. Imitate the model:

Model: (a) Whence did you come?

πόθεν ἦλθες;

(b) They asked him whence he had come.

ἐπηρώτων αὐτὸν πόθεν ἦλθεν. (Indicative)

(c) ἐπηρώτων αὐτὸν πόθεν ἔλθοι. (Optative)

1. (a) Where are you going?

ποῦ πορεύῃ;

(b) They asked him where he was going.

____

(c) ______________________________

2. (a) Who ate the fruit?

τίς ἔφαγεν τὸν καρπόν;

(b) They asked him who ate the fruit.

____

(c) ______________________________

3. (a) Where did they go?

ποῦ ἐπορεύθησαν;

(b) They asked us where we went.

____

(c) ______________________________

4. (a) Who is eating the bread?

τίς ἐσθίει τὸν ἄρτον;

(b) They asked him who was eating the bread.

____

(c) ______________________________

5. (a) Who is this man?

τίς ἐστιν οὗτος;

(b) They asked us who this man was.

____

(c) ______________________________

Exercise 50-C: Study the models given, and translate the remaining English sentences into Greek, using the optative mood:

0. Model: God has filled us with joy.

ὁ θεὸς ἐπλήρωσεν ἡμᾶς χαρᾶς.

May God fill you with joy. (Retain the "tense")

ὁ θεὸς πληρώσαι ἡμᾶς χαρᾶς!

____

1. Model: It happened to the virgin according to the angel's word.

ἐγένετο τῇ παρθένῳ κατὰ τὸ ῥῆμα τοῦ ἀγγέλου.

May it happen to me according to thy word!

____

2. Model: The Lord gave them peace.

ὁ κύριος ἔδωκεν αὐτοῖς εἰρήνην.

May the Lord give you peace!

____

3. Model: Grace has been multiplied to us.

χάρις ἡμῖν ἐπληθύνθη.

May grace be multiplied to you!

____

4. Model: They believed in him gladly.

ἡδέως ἐπίστευσαν εἰς αὐτόν.

May they believe in him gladly!

---

5. Model: I saw him again.
πάλιν ἐγὼ εἶδον αὐτόν.

May I see him again!

Exercises to Appendix I

Exercise A: (Cf. Par. 390.) Put an X in the ( ) before the word which correctly completes the statement:

1. The ultima of πέμπω is ( ) long
( ) short
2. The penult of δοῦλος is ( ) long
( ) short
3. The penult of νόμου is ( ) long
( ) short
4. The antepenult of ἀπόστολος is ( ) long
( ) short
5. The antepenult of θηρίον is ( ) long
( ) short
6. The ultima of λόγος is ( ) long
( ) short
7. The ultima of λόγοις is ( ) long
( ) short
8. The ultima of λόγοι (nom. pl.) is ( ) long
( ) short
9. The ultima of λύοι (optative) is ( ) long
( ) short
10. The ultima of πέμπει is ( ) long
( ) short
11. The penult of χαίρω is ( ) long
( ) short

12. The ultima of τιμαί (nom. pl.) is ( ) long
( ) short

Exercise B: (Cf. Par. 391.) Put an X in the ( ) before the word which correctly completes the statement:

1. The ultima of ἀλήθεια is ( ) long
( ) short

2. The ultima of σῶμα is ( ) long
( ) short

3. The ultima of βασιλεία is ( ) long
( ) short

4. The ultima of γνῶσις is ( ) long
( ) short

5. The ultima of δοῦλοι is ( ) long
( ) short

6. The ultima of λῦσαι is ( ) long
( ) short

7. The ultima of γλώσσας is ( ) long
( ) short

8. The ultima of ἀνάλυσις is ( ) long
( ) short

9. The penult of πύργος is ( ) long
( ) short

10. The ultima of κήρυξ is ( ) long
( ) short

11. The ultima of πιστεύοι is ( ) long
( ) short

12. The ultima of πιστεύσαι is ( ) long
( ) short

Exercise C: (Cf. Par. 393.) In the paradigms below the nominative singular forms are correctly accented; write the correct accent in the remaining forms:

		1.	2.	3.
Sg.	N.	ἀπόστολος	οἶκος	νόμος
	G.	ἀποστολου	οἰκου	νομου
	D.	ἀποστολῳ	οἰκῳ	νομῳ
	A.	ἀποστολον	οἰκον	νομον
Pl.	N.	ἀποστολοι	οἰκοι	νομοι
	G.	ἀποστολων	οἰκων	νομων
	D.	ἀποστολοις	οἰκοις	νομοις
	A.	ἀποστολους	οἰκους	νομους

Exercise D: (Cf. Par. 394(1).) Same directions as for Exercise C:

		1.	2.	3.
Sg.	N.	χαρά	φωνή	θεός
	G.	χαρας	φωνης	θεου
	D.	χαρᾳ	φωνῃ	θεῳ
	A.	χαραν	φωνην	θεον
Pl.	N.	χαραι	φωναι	θεοι
	G.	χαρων	φωνων	θεων

D.	χαραις	φωναις	θεοις
A.	χαρας	φωνας	θεους

Exercise E: (Cf. Par. 394(2).) Same directions as for Exercise C:

	1.	2.	3.
Sg.N.	ναύτης	γλῶσσα	βασιλεία
G.	ναυτου	γλωσσας	βασιλειας
D.	ναυτῃ	γλωσσᾳ	βασιλειᾳ
A.	ναυτην	γλωσσαν	βασιλειαν
Pl.N.	ναυται	γλωσσαι	βασιλειαι
G.	ναυτων	γλωσσων	βασιλειων
D.	ναυταις	γλωσσαις	βασιλειαις
A.	ναυτας	γλωσσας	βασιλειας

Exercise F: (Cf. Par. 394(5b).) Same directions as for Exercise C:

	1.	2.	3.
Sg.N.	γνῶσις	πίστις	ἀνάλυσις
G.	γνωσεως	πιστεως	ἀναλυσεως
D.	γνωσει	πιστει	ἀναλυσει
A.	γνωσιν	πιστιν	ἀναλυσιν
Pl.N.	γνωσεις	πιστεις	ἀναλυσεις
G.	γνωσεων	πιστεων	ἀναλυσεων
D.	γνωσεσιν	πιστεσιν	ἀναλυσεσιν
A.	γνωσεις	πιστεις	ἀναλυσεις

Exercise G: (Cf. Par. 394(4).) In the spaces provided, write the remaining forms of the adjective καλός, correctly accented:

	Masculine	Feminine	Neuter
Sg.N.	καλός	καλή	καλόν
G.	______	______	______
D.	______	______	______
A.	______	______	______
Pl.N.	______	______	______
G.	______	______	______
D.	______	______	______
A.	______	______	______

Exercise H: (Cf. Par. 394(4).) In the spaces provided, write the remaining forms of the adjective δίκαιος, correctly accented (for the accent of the neuter plural, nominative and accusative, cf. Par. 394(3)):

	Masculine	Feminine	Neuter
Sg.N.	δίκαιος	δικαία	δίκαιον
G.	______	______	______
D.	______	______	______
A.	______	______	______
Pl.N.	______	______	______
G.	______	______	______
D.	______	______	______
A.	______	______	______

Exercise I: (Cf. Par. 395.) In the spaces provided, write the forms of the present indicative, active and passive, of the verb ἐγείρω, correctly accented:

	Active	Passive (or Middle)
Sg.1.	____________	____________
2.	____________	____________
3.	____________	____________
Pl.1.	____________	____________
2.	____________	____________
3.	____________	____________

Exercise J: (Cf. Par. 395.) In the spaces provided, write the forms of the imperfect indicative, active and passive, of the verb ἄγω, correctly accented:

	Active	Passive (or Middle)
Sg.1.	____________	____________
2.	____________	____________
3.	____________	____________
Pl.1.	____________	____________
2.	____________	____________
3.	____________	____________

Exercise K: (Cf. Par. 395.) In the spaces provided, write the required imperative forms of the verb λούω, correctly accented:

	Present Active	Present Midd. or Pass.	Aorist Active	Aorist Middle
Sg.2.				
3.				
Pl.2.				
3.				

Exercise L: (Cf. Par. 397.) In the spaces provided, write the (hypothetical) uncontracted forms and the contracted forms of the verbs indicated, as required, all correctly accented:

Present Indicative of ποιέω:

	Active		Middle or Passive	
	Uncontracted	Contracted	Uncontracted	Contracted
Sg.1.				
2.				
3.				
Pl.1.				
2.				
3.				

Imperfect Indicative of ἀγαπάω:

	Active		Middle or Passive	
	Uncontracted	Contracted	Uncontracted	Contracted
Sg.1.				
2.				

3.	____	____	____	____
Pl.1.	____	____	____	____
2.	____	____	____	____
3.	____	____	____	____

Present Subjunctive of πληρόω:

	Active		Middle or Passive	
	Uncontracted	Contracted	Uncontracted	Contracted
Sg.1.	____	____	____	____
2.	____	____	____	____
3.	____	____	____	____
Pl.1.	____	____	____	____
2.	____	____	____	____
3.	____	____	____	____

Exercise M: (Cf. Par. 400.) Copy the expressions below in the spaces provided, altering or adding accents if necessary; if no alteration or addition is necessary, simply put a check mark in the blank space:

1. ὁ μαθητὴς μου. ____
2. ὁ προφήτης μου. ____
3. οἱ προφῆται μου. ____
4. ὁ ἀπόστολος μου. ____
5. ὁ ἀδελφὸς ἐστιν. ____
6. ὁ νόμος ἐστιν. ____

7. γράφει σοι. ______________________________

8. ἔγραψε σοι. ______________________________

9. οἱ νόμοι εἰσιν δίκαιοι. ______________________________

10. δίκαιοι ἐσμεν. ______________________________

11. γεγραμμένα εἰσιν ταῦτα. ______________________________

12. ὁ διάκονος μου ἐστιν πιστός. ______________________________

____

13. τοῦτο σῶμα μου ἐστιν. ______________________________

14. τοῦτο ἐστιν σῶμα μου. ______________________________

15. οὐκ εἰμι ἀπόστολος. ______________________________

16. οὐκ ἐστιν μαθητής. ______________________________

17. ἐστε φίλοι μου. ______________________________

18. ἐστιν βασιλεύς. ______________________________

Exercise N: (Cf. Par. 400.) In each of the expressions below a form of the indefinite pronoun occurs; copy the expressions in the spaces provided, following the directions given for Exercise M:

1. διάκονος τις. ______________________________

2. διάκονοι τινες. ______________________________

3. δῶρον τι. ______________________________

4. δῶρα τινα ______________________________

5. εἴδομεν ἄνδρα τινα. ______________________________

6. ἄνδρας τινας εἴδομεν. ______________________________

7. ἀπὸ τόπων τινων. ______________________________

8. ἄνθρωποι τινες εἰσιν ἐκεῖ. ______________________________

____

9. ἄνθρωπος τις ἐστιν ἐκεῖ. ______________________________

10. ἄρτον τισιν ἔδωκεν. ______________________________

11. ἔδωκεν τινι ἄρτον. ______________________________

12. ὁ υἱὸς χήρας τινος. ______________________________

13. ὁ υἱὸς χήρας τινος τέθνηκεν. ______________________________

____

14. ὁ υἱὸς γυναικὸς τινος. ______________________________

15. ὁ βασιλεὺς πόλεως τινος. ______________________________

16. νόμους τινας ἔγραψαν. ______________________________

17. τινες τῶν γραμματέων. ______________________________

18. πρὸς τινας ἐλεύσεται. ______________________________

Exercise O: (Cf. Par. 398.) If the indefinite pronouns in the expressions in Exercise N are changed into interrogative pronouns, what alterations must be made in the accents? Make the changes, writing the altered forms below (write the Greek question mark after each expression:

1. ______________________________
2. ______________________________
3. ______________________________
4. ______________________________
5. ______________________________
6. ______________________________
7. ______________________________
8. ______________________________

9. ______________________________
10. ______________________________
11. ______________________________
12. ______________________________
13. ______________________________
14. ______________________________
15. ______________________________
16. ______________________________
17. ______________________________
18. ______________________________